What's the Difference?

Building on Autism Strengths, Skills, and Talents in Your Classroom

Amanda Yuill

Pembroke Publishers Limited

© 2021 Pembroke Publishers
538 Hood Road
Markham, Ontario, Canada L3R 3K9
www.pembrokepublishers.com

Funded by the Government of Canada
Financé par le gouvernement du Canada | Canadä

Library and Archives Canada Cataloguing in Publication

Title: What's the difference? : building on autism strengths, skills, and talents in your
classroom / Amanda Yuill.

Names: Yuill, Amanda, author.

Identifiers: Canadiana (print) 20210149337 | Canadiana (ebook) 20210149396 |
ISBN 9781551383484 (softcover) | ISBN 9781551389509 (PDF)

Subjects: LCSH: Autistic children—Education (Elementary)

Classification: LCC LC4717 .Y95 2021 | DDC 371.94—dc23

Editor: Kat Mototsune
Cover Design: John Zehethofer
Typesetting: Jay Tee Graphics Ltd.

Printed and bound in Canada
9 8 7 6 5 4 3 2 1

Contents

Introduction

He did not come into my music classroom the whole year. Even when we had an electric campfire, complete with marshmallows, this little autistic boy in Grade 3 wandered the halls with his educational assistant. The following year I taught physical education. He would come into the gym; however, he would often run away. His homeroom teacher and I discussed it with him and decided that I would offer him a small amount of chips to eat if he would stay in the gym the whole period. The very next class, he stayed in the gym the whole period and I offered him some Pringles chips. He took one look at them, said, "Those aren't Lays," and walked away. Apparently, I still had a lot more to learn about teaching this little boy.

What's the difference between teaching our students and teaching our autistic students? Not much. This book offers strategies to be used to teach all students that are designed to specifically help our autistic students. Many of our autistic students have strengths, skills, talents, and interests that lend themselves to aid in learning. Some common ones are attention to detail, detailed memory, and skills with math and computers. For example, some autistic students will remember exactly what was said and will be able to repeat it for the whole class—whether I said it under my breath or not! As we explore each student's strengths, we can help all our students to learn, and—more than that—to have fun learning.

Every child can learn. When we say an autistic child cannot learn, what has really happened is that we, ourselves, have learned the limits of our patience and imagination. I believe that once we can figure out how someone learns and their strengths, everyone will be revealed to be quite intelligent. We have simply not been taught how to see everyone as smart. My father failed two grades and dropped out of high school at age 18, still in Grade 10. Later in life, he finished high school and went on to college; he became a mechanic and eventually an engine builder with the Toronto Transit Commission. He also got his private pilot's licence and flew planes as a hobby. He had severe dyslexia, which had never been diagnosed. He grew up believing he was dumb. Thankfully, he grew to understand that he was, in fact, smart. One time in college, he got 85% on a chemistry test. He accused the teacher of marking the tests with more lenience for the students in night school, because he simply couldn't believe he could receive such a good mark on his own. The teacher was offended and told him in no uncertain terms that he had in fact, earned that mark. So you see, he was learning that he was, in reality, smart.

Are we, as a society, willing to get rid of labels that call people dumb, stupid, slow, etc.? Are we willing to accept that everyone is intelligent if we can simply unlock their abilities? This will not take anything away from those who have been traditionally labeled intelligent. In fact, it will allow us to finally see, understand, and recognize the contributions of those who learn differently. It is time to end discrimination against those who learn in atypical ways. It is time for real and drastic changes in behaviors and attitudes. It is time to accept autistic people as an important, necessary, and beneficial part of our society, who make contributions we would not otherwise have.

The purpose of this book is to describe how to teach autistic students integrated into mainstream classrooms, especially when the teacher has little or no special education training. There has been an increase in the number of autistic students in mainstream classrooms and this number will continue to rise. This would be okay if there was enough support offered to students and teachers to help these students learn; however, there is often very little support offered to the teacher. Each autistic student is unique, so this book offers many different strategies, tips, and tools in an effort to provide at least a few that will work with each student. It goes through the ways you can prepare to have autistic students in your class.

It's two weeks before school starts and the principal tells you that you will have an autistic student in your class this year. What do you do, besides feel very anxious because this is a new experience for you? Well, there are many ways can you can **prepare yourself, your classroom, and your students.** The first thing might be to talk with the student's parents and see what they have to say—they are the experts, of course. Your goal is to work with them, to be partners with them. You will want to prepare your classroom environment—both the physical aspects and the atmosphere. One way to do this is to use the Universal Design for Learning (UDL). This means that, if one student needs a modification, that modification is used in the classroom for everyone. For example, if a student is sensitive to loud noises, instead of giving them noise-cancelling headphones, we keep the classroom atmosphere calm and quiet. You can also prepare a lesson plan for the first day that makes sure everyone feels welcomed into your classroom, introduces autism, and sets out how you, as a class, will treat everyone.

"When you've met one autistic person, you've met one autistic person" is a common phrase in the autistic community, first coined by Dr. Stephen Shore. It indicates that everyone is different. Everyone is unique. Therefore, it will take some time to **get to know your autistic student** and how they learn. It might help if you learn some common patterns of thinking in autistic people. Of course, it's impossible to know all the many different patterns of thinking, but common patterns are presented by Dr. Temple Grandin, an autistic scientist and professor who has researched autistic learning patterns for many years. For example, picture thinkers easily remember pictures of places they have been. I am not a picture thinker. I can hardly remember where I parked my car! It might also be useful to understand common sensory issues experienced by autistic children. As you get to know your autistic students, you can adapt the classroom atmosphere to make the experience more pleasurable for them and for the rest of your students.

As a teacher, your main focus is to **help your students learn**. One year we had a worm terrarium in my Kindergarten classroom because the students were really interested in worms. I was thankful that the worms were still alive the day we released them back into the wild! Everything we did in class those two weeks had something to do with worms. When we are asking autistic children to do schoolwork we can use a similar strategy. They often have areas of deep and sustained interest. Incorporating those interests into everyday classroom activities can help these students enjoy learning. Sometimes these interests are a part of these students' autistic genius. I taught one student who knew the birthday of everybody in the school and could tell you what day of the week you were born on (assuming you told the truth about how old you were). He really enjoyed when we used this strength in our lessons.

Emotional regulation is difficult for many children to learn, and it is no different for autistic children. It's important to learn what it is that triggers them to lose their ability to regulate their emotions. For that matter, it's important to learn your own triggers, the things that make it difficult to regulate your emotions. For example, you might be triggered when you've already said yes when they called your name but they continue to call your name five more times before telling you what it is they want. It has been traditionally thought that when students are not doing what the teacher is asking, it is because they are rebellious or don't want to do what we have asked of them. For many autistic students, this is just not the case. The truth is they would love to do what we are asking, but their anxiety prevents them from doing so. Help your students by having a calm classroom atmosphere and by teaching them many ways they can stay calm. More than just staying calm, we want them to build self-esteem. It is not simply the presence of emotional regulation, but also the presence of self-esteem that is the mark of emotionally healthy students.

The term "minimally verbal" is preferred to "nonverbal," which is often not accurate. Even if our students do not use words to communicate, most still use sounds, which are verbal. Also, many autistic students become more and more verbal as they get older.

Simply because you have a minimally verbal student in the classroom does not mean that they are minimally communicative. I'm sure you can think of many instances when students communicated without the use of words and made a fairly big impression. Many students may already have other ways of communicating; for example, they might know a bit of sign language and you may need to learn a bit of sign language as well. Or students may have high-tech aids; for example, they use Google Voice Typing, as I am doing right now. Other times, we, as teachers, need to find aids to help communication. I find that once we **help students communicate**, there is a decrease in challenging behaviors.

One of the defining aspects of autism is that it hinders the development of relationships. Therefore, we need to **help students learn social skills**. It can be beneficial to use social stories that demonstrate how to act in a certain social situation. Another way to help students make friends is by having peer groups. Social skills include living skills. This means that we take the things we learn in school and apply them to our everyday lives. Students enjoy trips to the grocery store to learn how to make change, how to budget, and how to choose healthy food. I remember teaching a Kindergarten student how to pull up his pants that were too tight. We used the pull, wiggle, and repeat method. Ultimately, we want to help prepare students for college, university, a job, or whatever comes after school. Grandin (2020) encourages us to teach our autistic students to use the back door to get a job. A young autistic man I know ended up getting a job in computers out of a platform he created.

Of course, we also want to **help our autistic students stay safe** in school. What do we do when they run away? When they run down the street? When they run home? The answer? RUN!!! Okay, that's only part of the answer—the first part! It's important to find strategies that work for each individual student to keep them and others safe when they feel they want to run, or when they harm themselves or others. It's important to find the root of the problem. Perhaps it is bullying. Many autistic students are bullied. Sometimes they are bullied because of inappropriate behavior they are displaying; for example, sexual touching. I'm pretty sure they didn't teach me what to do about that in teachers college! As with all students, autistic students might be bullied because they are different from other students. Many autistic children try to fit in by masking their autism. But when autistic people ignore who they are for too long and try to appear neuro-typical, it can lead to autistic burnout. It is important for us to teach not only our autistic students, but all of our students, that it is okay to be different and unique—to be themselves!

1

Preparing for Autistic Students

I spoke to the mother of one of my Kindergarten students about two weeks into school. I told her that I had noticed that her son didn't speak very much in school. She said that it was a symptom of his autism. She and I were both surprised that I didn't know her son was autistic. Because he had just been diagnosed and they did not yet have the doctor's report, it wasn't in his student record. Her husband was supposed to tell me on the first day of school but didn't. I felt bad, because I was sure her husband was going to be in trouble when he got home that day!

Autism as a Way of Being

If you haven't had an autistic student in your class, you probably will soon. It's good to know something about autism and have some background information in order to be prepared to teach these students. Autism Speaks is an organization that advocates for and supports autistic individuals and their families. On their website (https://www.autismspeaks.org/what-autism), autism is defined as, "a broad range of conditions characterized by challenges with social skills, repetitive behaviors, speech and nonverbal communication." For example, in your class, you may have an autistic student who has a hard time making friends or understanding social cues. You may have a student who rocks back and forth or repeats certain phrases. Autism can include, but is not limited to, Asperger syndrome, Pervasive Development Disorder—Not Otherwise Specified (PDD-NOS), and autism. It is good to keep this in mind when reading student records, since a student might have a diagnosis on the autism spectrum that is not specifically called autism. In fact, more than a century ago, Hans Asperger, after whom Asperger's Syndrome is named, said, "Once one has learnt to pay attention to the characteristic manifestations of autism, one realizes that they are not at all rare" (Asperger, 1991, p. 39). It is important to mention here that, while autism has traditionally been mostly diagnosed in boys, recently there has been progress in recognizing autism in girls and the varying symptoms most commonly displayed

See page 112 for a list of people I interviewed to prepare for writing this book.

by girls. So if it seems like there are more autistic students in classrooms recently, it is due to improved diagnosis (PricewaterhouseCoopers, 2006). In the schools where I work, it is common to have one or two autistic students in a class. Now that we know there will be an increase of autistic students integrated into our classes, what can we do?

Eva Kyriakides, Special Education Advisory Committee Chair for a board of education, states, "Integration is excellent with the proper supports, and that's key—that's the part we are missing and not something school boards can address easily." So, if integration is excellent, but we don't have the proper supports, what can teachers do to prepare? One of the most important things we can do is to make sure that we have a good attitude, without bias, toward autistic students.

There has been a long history of discrimination against autistic people. Science writer and activist Steve Silberman (2015, p. 1132) tells the story of Bill, the real person on whom the character Rain Man was based (*Rain Man* is a 1988 movie with Tom Cruise and Dustin Hoffman—definitely worth seeing!).

> He had never been taught how to tell time or handle money, and had never received proper dental care. Like the other inmates, he was paid the equivalent of 30 cents to $1.50 a month—redeemable only in goods from the hospital store—for backbreaking work like pushing food trolleys through the miles of dank tunnels that connected the various areas of the hospital (Silberman, 2015, p. 356).

Bill had been declared a ward of the state against his mother's wishes and she was not allowed to take him out of the hospital for the feeble-minded. Brown and Radford (2015, p. 11) reveal that in Canada from the 1920s to the 1940s there were forced sterilization programs for institutionalized autistic patients.

This discrimination, although perhaps less blatant, is still around today. Paula Kluth and Patrick Schwarz (2008, p. 61), state, "Sometimes opportunities are taken away from a student with autism under the guise of safety or simply because the individual has a disability. This can result in subtle to very blatant discrimination." Joseph Hancock, a young adult on the autism spectrum, shares that, in his experience, many people think that *autistic* means "idiot," sometimes because he doesn't like talking. He says that it is important for people to realize that, in many autistic brains, one part of the brain is larger than another. Although he may not be very talkative, he is excellent at math, statistics, numbers, and patterns. Michelle Dawson (2004) asserts that if your goal is to extinguish autistic behavior, your goal is to extinguish autistic people. The sterilization programs have perhaps simply taken a new form.

Of course, as teachers, we want to help our students. We want to treat them well. How do we do that? I suggest we ask the autistic community themselves how they would like to be treated. John Elder Robison (2007, p. 5) says, "Asperger's is not a disease. It's a way of being. There is no cure, nor is there a need for one. There is, however, a need for knowledge and adaptation..." This is echoed by Oliver Sacks when he talks about a family of four, all of whom are autistic. They had come to feel that their autism was a "whole mode of being and an identity." In fact, it was more than just an identity, but also something of which to be proud. Sacks cites Grandin, who says that people with autism, dyslexia, and other cognitive differences could make contributions to society that so-called normal people are incapable of making. She says that if she could snap her fingers and be non-autistic, she would not, because it would not be her. Therefore, it is important that we, as educators, don't treat autism as a disease, but as another way of

Donna Williams (1996) reminds us, "Some [individuals] really need to ask themselves whether they might not be able to have a little more tolerance of eccentricity than they already have, not just regarding the 'autistic' people in their care, but in themselves as well" (p. 229).

being. In fact, I wonder if it is time to drop the word, "Disorder" from Autism Spectrum Disorder and just call it the Autism Spectrum.

If we treat autism not as a disease, but as a way of being, it leads us to accommodate our autistic students in the way they need in order to learn. It also involves seeing autism as a strength. As Kluth and Schwarz say, "To put it another way, we feel that talking and thinking about students in ways that are more positive, hopeful, and strengths-based is not only more kind but also more helpful." (2008, p. 125) Everyone can learn. Everyone has strengths. It's simply a matter of getting to know our students and unlocking those strengths—unlocking the way they learn. Yes, this can take more time. Yes, this can be more difficult. Yes, we do need to find a balance. However, we didn't become teachers to have an easy job. We became teachers to help children. All children.

Your Autism Vocabulary List

> ### A Note on Terminology
>
> "Autistic students" is used instead of "students with autism" because the autistic community prefers this terminology. Saying "students with autism" can seem to indicate that autism is a disease, and there is no scientific basis for this (Michelle Dawson, 2004). However, every individual on the autism spectrum needs to decide for themselves the terminology they prefer. It is the intention in this book to honor this through the language used.

The first time you speak to the parents of your autistic student you might think that they are both doctors. They use technical vocabulary, acronyms, and words you don't know, and they talk as though you are following along. This is because autism has its own vocabulary. It helps to know some of the terminology before you start teaching your autistic students. And so, reminiscent of when you were in Grade 5, here is your vocabulary list. Don't worry, I won't make you write out the words 10 times each and then use them in a sentence. Just a note, there are many more words than I have included here that could come up in discussions about autism or autistic students. There is always new terminology as autistic culture and research advances. This is just an overview of the more common words you will hear.

Words Describing Autism

ASD, or Autism Spectrum Disorder. "Autism spectrum disorders (ASD) are complex neurodevelopmental conditions, characterized by a range of difficulties including impairments in social cognition, deficits and delays in language and communication abilities and restricted interests or activities, as expressed by repetitive patterns of behavior" (Cantiani et al., 2016). The important thing here is that it is a range. Autism comes in a spectrum. A BIG spectrum. Although this definition indicates a range of deficits and delays, there is also, and more importantly, a range of strengths and talents. In fact, Joseph Ronca, who teaches an autism class, says that, in his opinion, the differences between his autistic students are greater than the differences between autistic students and neurotypical students (see below for the definition of neurotypical—this is just a teaser).

Asperger syndrome or *Asperger's.* "An autism spectrum disorder (ASD) marked by impaired social interactions and limited repetitive patterns of behavior, interests, and activities" (Psychology Today). The main difference between autism and Asperger's is that children with Asperger's do not have significant delays with language. Though this term is still widely used, it is no longer an official diagnosis.

Aspie. Slang that people with Asperger syndrome use to refer to themselves.

Autism. See ASD

High-Functioning. This term usually describes students who are able to function well in life most of the time. People with a diagnosis of Asperger syndrome are usually considered high-functioning. This term is also mostly obsolete. Kyriakides explains that labelling a student high-functioning can confuse teachers. These students are intelligent and yet still can have poor emotional function (e.g., they can understand algebra but not why it's important to refrain from telling their mother she gained weight), which can lead to the student being overwhelmed and experiencing a sensory correction (see *Meltdown* below).

Low-Functioning. This usually refers to an individual who is minimally verbal or has severe challenges. This term is quickly becoming obsolete, as it can hinder a student's progress. Rob Lovering Spencer, a Special Education teacher who has taught autistic students for years, relates how he taught one student who was functionally mute when she came to his class and says, "Now, you can't stop her from talking." According to Silberman (2015 p. 425), Grandin didn't speak until she was three years old, and now she is very successful. He also tells of a mother who preferred to call her son High-Octane Boy so that she wasn't constantly defining him in terms of his deficits (Silberman, 2015, p. 79). Many autistic people who are considered low-functioning in their youth become high-functioning later in life.

On the Spectrum. Short for *on the autistic spectrum.* It is basically a synonym for autistic. For example, if someone says, "My son is on the spectrum and he always corrects his teacher's math," they mean that their son is autistic (and better than the teacher at math).

PDD-NOS. Pervasive Developmental Disorder—Not Otherwise Specified, the diagnosis used for "children or adults who are on the autism spectrum but do not fully meet the criteria for another ASD such as autistic disorder (sometimes called "classic" autism) or Asperger syndrome" (Autism Speaks Canada). For example, a student might have good social skills instead of the limited social skills traditionally a large part of an autism diagnosis, and still receive a PDD-NOS diagnosis.

Words Describing Common Characteristics of Autistic People

Echolalia. The way that autistic people sample the speech they hear around them and repurpose it for their own use (Silberman, 2015, p. 46). Young autistic students will often repeat back to you what you just said. Their whole vocabulary might be comprised of lines from the movie *Frozen.* No, thank you, I don't want to build a snowman.

Meltdown. I'm guessing I don't have to define this term. However, in an effort to use more positive terminology in this book, I will be using *sensory correction* instead of *meltdown* (as recommended by Lovering Spencer). One of the most common causes of meltdowns is a student being overloaded with sensory issues. The meltdown is often a way to try to restore the balance in these sensory issues.

Stimming. Short for *self-stimulation.* It is most often a repetitive body motion; for example, flapping hands or rocking. When neurotypical students do this, we call it fidgeting. Researchers have found that autistic people stim to reduce anxiety and because it feels good; it, in fact, facilitates learning by allowing the student to think about the matter at hand instead of thinking about how to stop stimming (Silberman, 2015, p. 48).

Words Describing Therapy

ABA. Applied Behavior Analysis, "a set of principles based on the science of behavior that are used to change behavior" (Children's Support Solutions). ABA is a very controversial therapy for autistic children that aims to increase functional skills and decrease problematic behavior by using rewards and punishment. The autistic community mostly hates it and it is spoken of as punitive and abusive (Kohn, 2020). Some parents love it because, for example, it stopped their child from habitual self-harm. There is much research on the benefits and deficits of ABA.

DSM-5. Diagnostic and Statistical Manual of Mental Disorders, 5th ed, the rather large book used by doctors to diagnose autism (and by their children to hold the door open). While you might not hear parents or teachers of autistic students talk about this book, if you do any research about autism, you will certainly come across it.

IAS. Independent Activity Schedule, a set of pictures or words that signal a child to complete a group of activities (Surrey Place). It enables children to do activities independently with minimal supervision. (That means, as the teacher, you can finally sneak a snack).

IBI. Intensive Behavioral Intervention uses the same principles as ABA for treatment, designed to improve key learning skills in the areas of cognitive, language, and social development with the goal of increasing the rate of learning (Surrey Place). As it is based on ABA, it is also controversial. In Ontario, ABA is offered to parents to help the child learn a particular skill. IBI is offered to help a child catch up to their peers. ABA or IBI therapists could come into a school to work with a child. Parents might ask you to follow a particular routine learned through ABA/IBI in order for their child to acquire a skill and, whenever possible, I do this, as it usually benefits the student and me.

As teachers, we are not expected to do ABA or IBI therapy, as we are not trained in their use.

Words Describing the World from an Autistic Point of View

Neurotypical. A person who is not autistic or does not have other developmental differences (e.g., dyslexia). This phrase was first coined by Autism Network International (ANI), an autistic-run advocacy organization for autistic people.

Neurodiversity. The idea that differences in the brain are normal, not diseases or disorders. This includes the idea that we are all different and we all have strengths and weaknesses. Embracing the concept of neurodiversity can help reduce the stigma around children who think or learn differently. In an effort to advance this idea, Grandin uses engineering words instead of medical terms when talking about autism in her seminars (Leading Edge Seminars, 2020).

Neurodiversity Is Cool!

The year I was 15, I was very sick. I had a lot of stomach pain and we didn't know why. I went to a lot of doctors and had many *unpleasant* tests done. The doctors couldn't figure out why I was sick, and in the end told me it was all in my head. I was very upset. However, my mom believed me and she decided to put me on an elimination diet. It turned out I had food allergies. I didn't need a pill; I needed someone to believe me. In our classrooms, our autistic students don't need a pill in order to be cured of autism; they need a teacher who believes in them. You are that teacher.

In the past, autism was seen only in light of its deficits and difficulties. Having a neurodiverse classroom means that we acknowledge that everyone learns in a different way, has strengths, and makes contributions. We are not trying to make everyone fit into the same mold—instead, we are enjoying the variety. We are helping students not only to accept differences, but also to embrace them. More than this, we are trying to take away the idea of *us vs. them*. They *are* us. I love what Robison says about this:

> When I wrote *Look Me in the Eye*, I wanted to show readers what it was like to grow up feeling like a freak or a misfit. I thought my book would show how people with Asperger's are different from everyone else. To my great surprise, my book actually shows the opposite: Deep down, people are very much the same. (Robison, 2007, p. 284)

When we can show that stimming and fidgeting are the same thing, when we can show our students (and ourselves) that our differences are shallow and our similarities are deep, it becomes easier to embrace neurodiversity because we realize that we really need each other. Consider this:

> When "*diversity becomes the norm*" pupils have been reported to feel more able to face the challenges and embrace the opportunities of the mainstream school environment. Participation is achieved when there is a sense of normalcy, and the diagnosis of ASD ceases to be a person's main attribute. (Krieger et al., 2018, p. 20)

Good speech, you may think, but how do I do that? One of the main things we need to do as teachers is to help students understand that we will not be treating everyone the same. Instead, we will be giving each student what they need to succeed. "But that's not fair!" the students' war cry rises. *Fair* is *very* important to them! We need to help students change their mindset and their perspective on this. We need to show them that *fair* is not getting the same help as everyone else, but instead is everyone getting what they need in order to learn. Janice Cook, who has been a child and youth worker and therapist working with autistic children, says it is helpful when a teacher really emphasizes diversity and that the classroom is a safe place for everyone. Gill Lea, a vice-principal, agrees. She says it is important to make sure the students know that what is outstanding for one person might not be outstanding for another person. I taught physical education to a Grade 7/8 class and a Grade 6/7/8 autistic class at the same time. One class we played a game and one of the autistic students won the game for his team. While he didn't exactly follow the rules, he followed the rules as best he could. To their credit, the Grade 7/8 class congratulated him on his win! At its best, neuro-

See page 25 for a checklist for Preparing for Autistic Students.

16

diversity in the classroom allows us all to "learn how to use [our] uniqueness to [our] advantage and find [our] place in the world" (Plank & Grover, 2004).

One for All and All for One

Kyriakides tells the story of an autistic girl who brought a cushion and a weighted stuffie (little-kid slang for a stuffed animal) to her Kindergarten class to help her sit in place and be comfortable. Other students started asking why they didn't have a cushion and a stuffie at school. So the teacher sent home a note inviting parents to send a cushion and a stuffie to school with their child. The result was that the cushion identified each child's space. If they were on their cushion, they were in their own space. The students became more comfortable and less fidgety, and they were better behaved in assemblies and in the classroom. Now I'm feeling all nostalgic about my pink and grey teddy bear…

This story is a great example of the Universal Design for Learning (UDL). The principle behind UDL is that what is necessary for one is beneficial for all. For example, when it is snowing, clearing the ramp is necessary for a student with a wheelchair and beneficial for all students, as they can also use the ramp instead of the stairs to enter the school. (And personally, I appreciate not having to clear more stairs!) In the past, we have been taught to teach the average student and then assist those who need extra help. However, if we aim to teach those students who need more support or have more challenges, we will teach all children, and this leads to a supportive school culture.

The Physical Classroom

In setting up a UDL classroom, we help not only our autistic students, but also all of our students. There are many things we can do to create a great physical environment that is welcoming to autistic students and all students. Some autistic people have unusual sensory perception that can make noises, light, smells, and spaces feel intimidating and overwhelming and can hinder participation (Krieger et al., 2018, p. 14).

Traditionally, teachers have been encouraged to have fun, colorful classrooms in which almost every inch of the wall is covered. This can be very overwhelming for some students. In preparing a UDL classroom, it is best to keep posters and wallcovering to a minimum. Neutral and natural colors are best—think of the paint on hospital walls. You also want to keep the lighting low and to avoid music and loud or repetitive noises. You want to make sure that there are no overwhelming smells, including the shampoo or deodorant you use (FYI: organic does not always mean scent-free, and organic deodorant might not be as effective in odor elimination…). It is a good idea to speak with the student or parents before the first day of school to see if there are any sensory issues that you can address in your classroom before school starts. As you get to know your students, you can make adjustments to your classroom. For example, I know an autistic boy who cannot stand the smell of berries or yogurt, and the sensory distraction hinders his concentration. I often have strawberry yogurt for lunch, so I would make sure to eat it in the staffroom and not in the classroom. Or I could have chocolate pudding instead. Mmmm, chocolate…

Barbie Schiller, who has many years of experience working with autistic students in high schools as an educational assistant, emphasizes the strategic placing

"Six characteristics of successful inclusive schools emerged: committed leadership, democratic classes, reflective educator, supportive school culture, engaging and relevant curricula, responsive instruction." (Krieger et al., 2018 p. 13)

For more on sensory perception, see My Clothes Are Too Itchy! on p. 30.

of seating. You want to be able to help your students quickly if they need it, but you want it to be unobtrusive. She observes that it is good to have a kind, mature student sit next to a student who might need more help. Hancock agrees that seating is important. He says that he paid the most attention in class when he was at the back of the class, because then he knew people would not be looking over his shoulder. He needed to be sure that he had space to do his work; but if he looked like he was struggling, the teacher could come over and ask if he needed help. Kyriakides suggests that, along with strategic seating, having healthy, non-messy snacks that students can eat at any time available on their desks or in the classroom. This helps keep the students' blood sugar levels even, which can prevent behavior issues related to hunger and allow students (and teachers) to eat when they are hungry or tired.

Sari Lansimaki worked with autistic students and found that a visual schedule brought peace to her students' day because they knew what to expect and it was not as chaotic. Krieger et al. (2018, p. 15) found that, in autistic adolescents, order and predictability could be a "security blanket," making demands familiar. A visual schedule brings order and predictability to students, as it shows exactly what is going to happen throughout the day. The schedule is posted on the board or on every desk, with each activity marked with a picture beside the time. As each activity or period is completed, the picture can be taken down so that students know exactly where they are in the daily schedule. For younger students, it is a good idea to take a photo of students doing the activity and use that picture on the visual schedule.

Along with visual schedules, the use of a visual timer is recommended. You can use an online timer (I like www.online-stopwatch.com) or you can buy a physical countdown timer. Just be sure it is quiet. Some of them buzz. An annoying *buzzzzz*. Timers allow students to see how much time is left for an activity. It's a good idea to give a warning when there are five minutes left for an activity, as transitions are difficult for many students. You might want to start out giving many warnings: e.g., five minutes left, three minutes left, one minute left. Just be sure not to be like my grandma who, when she took us to the pool, used to yell, "Five minutes!" to let us know we would leave soon, and then talk to her friends for 30 minutes!

Sensory Corner

Did you ever buy a fridge, dishwasher, or oven when your children were young? What was their favorite part of your new appliance? That's right—the box! They made it into a house or a castle or a spaceship, and you were roped into helping. Or at least you helped cut out the windows so they wouldn't bleed all over your rug! Well, you can put those skills to good use again by making a sensory corner in your classroom. This is a space in your classroom where students can go to be alone, take a break, and calm down. You can set up a pup tent or simply put a blanket over two bookshelves. It can have headphones (so students can block out sound), fidget toys, bean bags, glow balls, glitter sticks, books, weighted vests, bubble-making materials, and pillows. Or it can be simple, with just a blanket, pillows, and books. As you get to know your students, you can change the sensory corner to tailor it to your class. Some schools have a separate room called a sensory room or a Snoezelen room. Similar to a sensory corner, it would have many items and activities for student to use to calm down.

Schoolwork

Besides the physical environment of the classroom, UDL also includes how we introduce schoolwork. A UDL paradigm boils down to offering choices for how students learn and how they demonstrate their learning. Just like some people prefer chocolate and some people prefer vanilla (chocolate is best, of course), students prefer to learn and show their learning in a variety of ways. We want to engage our students with multiple modalities to help them get excited about what we're teaching. For example, I might explain a new math concept, show an example, and then allow students to work with manipulatives; in this way, I have used oral, visual, and kinesthetic teaching methods. I might allow students to have the choice of showing their understanding of a history unit through a research paper, an oral presentation, a video, a detailed poster, or a historical fiction piece. Of course, many teachers already use these strategies in their classroom, but it is important to plan to teach all lessons with many different learning styles in mind and to offer a choice in most, if not all, classroom work. This takes some planning, but it is worth it because it lets students enjoy learning and feel more confident that they can do well. They really surprise me sometimes with the quality of work they produce and end up doing much more than I would have required if I made all the decisions instead of offering choice!

More on helping autistic students do schoolwork is presented in chapter 3.

The Teacher

Of course, as teachers, we are a big part of our classroom environments. Over and over, I have heard people say that it is important that we remain calm, no matter what is going on in the classroom. This builds trust with our students. Schiller reports that, even when one of her students threw a computer around the room, she remained calm. She recommends that you don't yell and don't act startled, but "step back and speak as calmly as your best inner actor can allow." Students need help de-escalating first, and then you can deal with the issue. This is more difficult than it sounds—and it sounds difficult. It is easier with practice, and I have found that role playing with other teachers really helps me prepare. If we are able to maintain our calm, the reward is that we will be able to help the student calm down instead of escalating into something more dangerous. Students are often more upset at the idea that they will be in trouble or that they have done something wrong than at what happened. We can reassure them that they are not in trouble and that we will work it out. (Being "in trouble" often means that someone will yell. We are not going to yell.) I remember there was a young student who would answer me only with one-word answers, while she would speak in sentences to the other educator in the room. I realized that I simply spoke too loudly for her. After that, when I spoke to her, I tried to remember to use my very quiet voice, something I don't do naturally. (I tend to be the loud, enthusiastic teacher.) And she started giving me longer answers!

Even though we provide different ways for students to learn, students still want to be treated the same as everyone else. If it looks like we are giving special treatment to one student, they might not accept the help. Krieger et al. (2018, p. 19) found that "Overt staff attention can be perceived as negative, as it accentuates the differences... Skilled support should be provided subtly and in the background to reduce the attention that adolescents with ASD get." *Give sneaky help* is the moral of the story here.

As much as possible, we want to use humor that our students understand to keep the classroom environment fun. Trina Meloche's daughter, Delilah, did not like gym; in fact, she would not go into the gym but would stand outside in the hallway. Her gym teacher would sing, "Hey, there Delilah, what's it like out there in the hallway?" Delilah would laugh and go into the gym to participate. So, let that inner entertainer come out! You know it's in there—all teachers have it. Use that song you've been practicing in the shower for your America's Got Talent audition!

What Do I Do on the First Day?

You're dressed nicely. The classroom looks good. You baked them cookies—no? Okay, so you bought them Timbits. You've practiced their names and put their desks in order. Now what? Your first day is going to be pretty much the same as all your other first days. Schiller recommends greeting autistic students with a friendly smile, having a matter-of-fact attitude about the expectations in your class, expecting students to do the work, and asking questions but not forcing them to answer. The main difference is going to be how you introduce autism to the class. "Many adolescents with ASD express the fear that disclosure of their autism may lead to negative reactions, or even result in stigmatization" (Krieger et al. 2018, p. 15). So you want to make sure you have spoken with the student and their parents first to find out how they want to handle it.

A good place to start is with the idea that we are all different. Mary Boff, a special education teacher with many years experience with autistic students, recommends an activity called Being Unique, for which students need to write four ways in which they are unique. The idea is to normalize diversity. If students and parents agree, Lovering Spencer has parents come into his classroom as guest speakers to help normalize autism; he finds this works for Kindergarten to Grade 6.

Many educators recommend starting with a book, such as *All Cats Have Asperger Syndrome* by Kathy Hoopmann, a picture book suitable for Kindergarten to Grade 12. Lea recommends *Same But Different: Teen Life on the Autism Express* by Holly Robinson Peete, RJ Peete and Ryan Elizabeth Peete for middle-school students. RJ is autistic and he, his sister, and his mother wrote about what it's like to be an autistic teenager, a sister of an autistic brother, and a mother of an autistic son. No matter what book you use, the idea is to introduce autism as one of the many ways children are unique, as Krieger et al. (2018, p. 19) assert that "sensitively handled disclosure can facilitate understanding, empathy, and positive relationships." When autistic students feel that differences are normalized, there is a greater chance of their participation and enjoyment of the class—even on the first day! (And they may even notice that you look nice, too!)

Parents as Partners

Silberman (2015, p. 49) tells the story of an autistic boy who loved the green Starbucks straws. When his mother had trouble getting enough straws herself, she started a group called L.U.S.T.—the League of Unrepentant Straw Thieves. Many friends and family members joined the group and gathered as many straws as they could for the boy. This is the kind of thing that parents of autistic children do all the time. They know their child, they love their child, and they simply want the best for them.

Leo Kanner, the first to propose autism as a diagnosis in 1943, also proposed that autism was the result of a cold, unloving mother (Silberman, 2015, p. 188). The idea that autism is caused by bad parenting continues today, even though, as Silberman points out (2015, p. 261), it has been proven that autism is a congenital condition based on genetics and neurology. Even so, parents of autistic children are constantly judged to be the cause of their child's problems. One parent, tired of being blamed for her child's behavior, blurted out, "I have two other children. Do you think I parented this child differently from the other two? If I could have 'fixed' him, I would have 'fixed' him a long time ago!" Just to be clear, this parent felt it was the teacher's strategies that needed fixing, not her child. Over and over, I hear stories from parents about teachers blaming them for the difficulties the teachers are having in class. We need to change this. WE NEED TO CHANGE THIS. Blame is not helpful and will not improve our situation.

Instead of blaming them, I propose we see parents as partners and work with them as a team, as many teachers already do. Kyriakides suggests that we sit down with parents and honestly hear what works for them at home, because they know their child's interests and triggers. She tells the story of a teacher who called and asked a parent for suggestions to help with her child in school; the parent, who was driving, pulled over and cried from happiness because it was such a difference from her normal interactions with teachers. Lea suggests that you discuss your goals for your student with their parents. Beth Cubitt, a mom of two autistic children, describes how one teacher would discuss with her what she, as the teacher, could have done differently when Beth's child had issues in the classroom. The point was not to blame the teacher, nor the child, nor the parents, but instead to find a good resolution to the issue. Together, they would work as a team to find a good solution when neither of them knew the answers. Meloche, a parent of two autistic children, comments that communication with high-school teachers and the special education department are important to her. When there are meetings about her children, she prefers to be informed and makes herself available as a resource to provide advice or strategies. For the most part, parents want to help. We, as teachers, can see parents as teammates and as a valuable resource to use to the benefit of our students, not to mention ourselves. No, I am not just angling for better Christmas gifts—but I will mention that baked goods and Amazon gift cards are my favorites…

Lovering Spencer explains that there are many autistic students whose families are new to the country and so they don't yet have resources or connections. Part of working with parents is providing them with resources in your area to help their child. For example, there may be Boy/Girl Scouts, cooking classes, sports programs, craft programs, respite care, or summer camps that accommodate autistic children. Lovering Spencer also encourages parents to keep trying to use different resources, as they will benefit their child in the long run, even if they are unsuccessful at the beginning. Let parents know that, even when it significantly bombs and they are no longer welcome at that cooking class after the flour and spider fiasco, they can try something else. Some programs will be a better fit than others.

Another way we can be on the same team as parents is to help them recognize when it would be beneficial for their child to see a doctor and get assessed. Emily Crafting, a parent of two autistic children, recognizes that parents don't always "put two and two together" and sometimes might need help. We, as teachers, might have concerns about a child but be unsure how to approach the child's parents. Sue Hucklebridge, an ASD specialist working with autistic students at Durham College, recommends that you let parents know what your experience is with the student, not simply tell parents you think their child is autistic. She recommends talking with the parent many times and slowly easing them into the idea of having their child assessed; with the approval of the principal, you can offer to write a letter, describing what you have been seeing, which the parents can take to their doctor. If the child is six years old or younger, you can also suggest the Nipissing District Developmental Screen (NDDS) website at www. ndds.ca for access to the Looksee Checklist, commonly known as the Nipissing Test. It is a quick survey of skills a child should master by a particular age, not a diagnostic tool or formal assessment. If there is a No answer to any of the questions, a follow-up with a health-care provider is advised. You have to sign up for the website, but it is not difficult and it is free. The idea is to help parents come to the realization that their child might need an assessment; also, that this is actually a really good, not a horrible, thing. Remember when you counted your child's fingers and toes when they were born? We need to act with compassion as we help parents assess their child and realize that they may need some extra help in their lives.

Lesson Plan: Introduction to Autism

The purpose of this lesson plan is to introduce autism to the class. This lesson plan is best done in the first few days of school or in the week before or after your new autistic student joins your class.

Before using this lesson plan, it is really important to speak with the autistic student and their parents about having a lesson to introduce autism to the class and to find out if they are comfortable with this plan. Would your autistic student like to help present the lesson? Would they like to be part of the class, or would they like to be absent when you present the lesson? Would the parents like to help present the lesson or would they like to observe? Is there anything specific the student or parents would like the class to know about autism or about their child?

Introductory Activity : KWL Chart

1. Prepare a KWL chart on chart paper or on the board.
2. Ask the class what they know about autism. Write their responses in the first column under K for *Know*.
3. Next, ask students what they want to know or wonder about autism. Write their responses in the second column, under W for *Want to know* or *Wonder*.

4. Explain that the third column is for what they learned about autism during this lesson. Tell students you will fill it out at the end of the lesson (or partway through the lesson, if you decide to do it on the go).

Empathy Activity: Experiencing

1. Explain that autistic students often have unusual sensory perception; this means that they may hear things louder than others, or see things as brighter than others, etc. Explain that you will do an activity to help students experience what it might feel like to have sensitive sensory perception.
2. Have students form pairs. Partner A is the student; Partner B is the experience. Explain to the students that you will be asking them mental math questions for one minute.
3. Partner A's job is to ignore their partner and answer the questions.
4. Partner B will need a feather and a flashlight (they can use the one on their phones). Or you can choose one student to go around with a powerful flashlight, shining it into the eyes of everyone who is Partner A.
5. Read out mental math questions in a very loud voice, while Partner B shines a light into Partner A's eyes every now and then. Partner B also tickles Partner A with the feather, just at the seams of their shirt, every now and then.
6. Have partners switch so that the partner who was the student becomes the experience and the partner who was the experience becomes the student.
7. Explain that you spoke loudly because autistic students often hear noises as louder than normal. You had a light shone in their eyes because often lights are too bright for autistic students. You had them tickled with a feather because often the seams of clothing are too itchy for autistic students.
8. Ask students how the experience was for them. Ask them if it was hard to try to answer mental math questions when your voice was too loud, the lights too bright, and their clothes too itchy.
9. Write down some of the answers in the third column of your KWL chart, under L, what they *Learned*.

Information Activity: Book Discussion

1. Explain to the class that Asperger syndrome is a type of autism. Introduce the book *All Cats Have Asperger Syndrome* by Kathy Hoopmann to the class.
2. Read the book aloud. If you do not have that book in your library, you can find videos of readings on YouTube.
3. Be sure to mention that each person who has autism is different, so not everything in the book is true about everyone who has Asperger syndrome.
4. Add to the third column of your KWL chart by asking students what they learned about Asperger syndrome from the book.
5. During the discussion, reinforce the idea that everyone is unique, not only those with Asperger syndrome or autism. Look for similarities between students and the cat in the story; e.g., some students don't like it when their schedule is changed.

Sharing Activity: Revisiting KWL

1. Have students get into the same pairs as in the Empathy Activity. Have them share with each other things they learned about autism during the lesson,

questions they might still have, or information they know about autism that wasn't covered.

2. Have a few of the pairs share what they talked about with the class. Encourage discussion.

3. If the autistic student and parents are comfortable, let the class know that you have an autistic student in your class and let them know who it is.

4. If possible, allow students to ask the autistic student questions.

Preparing for Autistic Students: Checklist

Autism as a Way of Being

- ☐ Understand what autism is, including doing research if necessary.
- ☐ Know that there has been historical discrimination against autistic people and it is still around today, including exclusion from school programs.
- ☐ Recognize that autism can be a strength; e.g., proficiency with numbers, computers, patterns, etc.

Neurodiversity

- ☐ Let students know that you will not be treating everyone the same way, but you will be giving each student what they need to succeed.
- ☐ Help students not only to accept differences, but also to embrace them.

The Classroom Environment

The Physical Classroom
- ☐ Keep posters and colors to a minimum.
- ☐ Keep lighting low.
- ☐ Avoid loud or repetitive noises.
- ☐ Avoid strong smells.
- ☐ Have an autistic student sit where they are comfortable in the class, but not too far from you.
- ☐ Allow students to snack anytime.
- ☐ Use a visual schedule.
- ☐ Use visual timers.
- ☐ Provide a sensory corner where students can go to calm down.
- ☐ Have a classroom pet.

Schoolwork
- ☐ Keep in mind various learning styles; e.g., visual, auditory, kinesthetic.
- ☐ Allow students to choose how they will be assessed; e.g. oral presentation, written report, detailed poster, etc.

The Teacher
- ☐ Stay calm to help de-escalate situations.
- ☐ Avoid the appearance of favoring autistic students or giving them special attention.
- ☐ Provide support subtly.
- ☐ Use humor.

The First Day

- ☐ Same as always: greet students with a friendly smile; be matter-of-fact about your expectations; ask questions but don't force answers.
- ☐ Start with the idea we are all different and the Being Unique activity.
- ☐ Speak with autistic student and their parents before the first day of school to find out how they would like autism introduced to the class.
- ☐ Ask parents of autistic student if they would like to be guest speakers to help normalize autism.
- ☐ Use read-alouds.

Parents as Partners

- ☐ Do NOT blame parents for their autistic child's behavior.
- ☐ Work with parents as a team.
- ☐ Ask parents what works for them at home and take what can be applied to the classroom.
- ☐ Work with parents to find answers to problems.
- ☐ Help families who are new to the country find resources.
- ☐ Slowly help families recognize that their child needs to see a doctor to be assessed.

Pembroke Publishers ©2021 *What's the Difference?* by Amanda Yuill ISBN 978-1-55138-348-4

2

Getting to Know Autistic Students

When You've Met One Autistic Person, You've Met One Autistic Person

Beth Cubitt says that her autistic daughter is a social butterfly, talking with everyone; her conversation does not make sense, but she loves to be around people. Beth's autistic son, on the other hand, is an introvert and loves to spend time in his room. Cubitt explains that autism is many things and that the absence of one characteristic in a child doesn't mean they are not autistic. As I have spoken with autistic people and parents and teachers of autistic children, I have heard this phrase over and over again: "When you've met one autistic person, you've met one autistic person." People don't like to be stereotyped. As teachers, we don't like to be stereotyped as people who wear sweaters for each holiday (although some teachers do this), and autistic people don't like to be stereotyped as introverts who like visual schedules (although some autistic people are introverts and do like visual schedules).

As difficult as it might be, Schiller encourages teachers not to make assumptions about our students because they're autistic. The worst thing we can do, she asserts, is to jump in and start talking to them, making demands, or asking questions. First, we have to build trust and have a relationship, then we can ask them to do something. Ronca agrees: one of his students prefers a specific black pen and doesn't like the other pens. Other autistic students in his class don't care. Every child is different—with or without a diagnosis or a label, everyone has their hangups, and it's important to understand that, Ronca asserts. One of my hang-ups is the young guys who try to race me while I'm swimming laps. I don't want to race; I just want to swim! So when this happens, I usually swim butterfly for a couple of lengths and leave them in the dust. Because I'm a calm, forgiving person. ;)

The expression, "When you've met one autistic person, you've met one autistic person" especially applies to autistic girls and women. Much of the research on autism was done with mainly male participants, and autism often presents differently in girls. Hucklebridge reveals this is because girls tend to use compensation skills to mask autism. Girls often mimic other girls—Hucklebridge's daughter chose two or three other girls and dressed like them. (I should have been as smart as that when I was a student. My style was a bit lacking…) Hucklebridge's daughter wasn't diagnosed until she was 22—it is common for girls on the autism spectrum to be diagnosed later in life. One high-school teacher says that, recently, some of her female students were diagnosed with autism in Grade 11 or 12, or even later in life. She believes this is because they fly under the radar more often than boys.

One of the more important issues to look into with our autistic student is if they have diagnoses besides autism. Nancy Lothian, an elementary and high-school educator who has worked with autistic students for more than 30 years, mentions that some of her students have also been diagnosed with Obsessive Compulsive Disorder, Oppositional Defiant Disorder, etc. Kyriakides observes that there are many autistic students in the gifted program. Moreover, nearly one third of the population diagnosed with autism is affected by epilepsy (Silberman, 2015, p. 185). This sort of information should be available in student records, so reading student records is important to do before the school year begins. If a student has a medical condition or a safety plan, it's crucial to be familiar with the action plan before the first day of school, before you're trying to figure out how their asthma puffer works and can't figure out which end goes in their mouth.

Besides reading the student record and talking with parents, talking with students one-on-one and building mutual trust is a good way to get to know our students, according to Tom, an adult on the autism spectrum. Meloche suggests having conversations with students to find out their quirks and what they like. Her son likes to doodle; one of his teachers discovered this and allowed him to draw when he was done with his work. Meloche asserts that it is necessary to know our students because then we are able to ascertain if a challenging behavior is simply typical or is due to the autism. We will handle the situation differently depending on our perception. Sunita Rathee, an educator in elementary schools, adds that each child behaves differently and it is important not to deal with all children the same way. We need to get to know our students so we can know which strategies work for each child. This is not news. Relationship is a very important part of teaching. Kluth and Schwarz (2008, p. 3) tell the story of Kip, an autistic student who loved farm equipment. His teacher Mr. Rye invited him to eat lunch together and asked him all about farm equipment. Kip had never had a teacher who shared his enthusiasm for farm equipment and he started looking forward to going to school, whereas previously he had begged to stay home. (The only thing I know about farm equipment is the company John Deere because it comes up in country songs a lot…)

See page 37 for a checklist for Getting to Know Autistic Students.

It sounds simple. Don't stereotype. Get to know our students. Be interested. The truth is, we have heard many times how autistic students don't like to be touched, don't look people in the eye, don't like loud noises etc. and we don't realize how much it has affected how we see our autistic students. Be intentional about getting to know each student as an individual so that stereotypes fall to the wayside and your students' personalities shine through.

There's Only One Way to Tie Shoes

It was inconceivable to me that there could be more than one way to play in the dirt, but there it was. Doug couldn't get it right. — John Elder Robison (2007, p. 7)

This is how Robison thought as a child with Asperger syndrome. However, many children think this way, not understanding that there are different points of view, and that more than one point of view can be valid. (Some adults haven't quite grasped this concept yet either.) Grandin (2013, p. 185) used to think that all autistic people thought in pictures, like she did, and all neurotypical people thought in words. However, as she talked with more and more autistic people, she realized that not all of them thought in pictures like she did. Over the years, she developed a theory about the various ways in which people think.

Grandin's theory maintains there are three categories of thinkers: word thinkers, picture thinkers, and pattern thinkers:

- Word thinkers are people who think in words and facts. These students are able to tell us what they are thinking. They also memorize words and dialogues easily. Word thinkers often love word games like Scrabble and Boggle!
- Picture thinkers think in images and have to translate what they are thinking into words in order to explain their thoughts. Picture thinkers want to create objects that they see in their imagination. They love hands-on activities like painting, cooking, or woodworking.
- Pattern thinkers are visual/spatial, abstract thinkers who see patterns everywhere. They think about the ways parts of objects fit together. They love Lego and other construction toys, and tools.

When we can figure out what kind of thinker our autistic students are, we can use their strengths, and we can work on areas that are more challenging for them in a way that they might understand. For example, I love word games, but I can't picture what the kitchen would look like in blue rather than yellow. I might use a computer program that allows me to change the color in pictures I take so that I can see what the kitchen will look like in blue. (I like it in yellow better.) In the classroom, I might give a picture thinker more time to explain what they did over the weekend as they translate their picture into words.

Cook says that, in her experience, some autistic high-school students have a "lawyer brain." They are very logical and fact-based, like Grandin's word thinkers. They will challenge the teacher if they think the teacher made a mistake or was inconsistent. The students are not trying to be disrespectful; they simply have a lawyer brain. They remember that you said you would give the class some free time next Friday and they are all too happy to remind you and remind you and remind you. Some students can get stuck on a fact when they know they are right or think they are right. This can be humbling for teachers. Cook suggests that you simply admit if you were not correct and go on. Otherwise, redirection can help; for example, "That's a really great point and we're going to continue with our lesson now. We can talk about it after that, if you need to."

Boff tells the story of an educational assistant who told her it was raining cats and dogs. The autistic child in the room ran to the window to see the cats and dogs. For some autistic students, abstract ideas, including idioms, can be difficult to understand. It's best just to use concrete language. This can also transfer over into high school. Lori Ann Welker's son cannot answer questions like, "Would you recommend this book to a friend?" because he doesn't know if his friend would like the book. Similarly, Kyriakides' son has difficulty with questions that require him to pretend he is someone else. For example, an assignment that asked him to pretend he was a farmer in the 1800s and talk about his life was hard for him, whereas reporting what life was like for farmers in the 1800s was much easier. Another difficult part of abstract thinking can be understanding the possible consequences of actions, especially when in new situations.

In communicating with autistic students, avoid the use of sarcasm in your humor. Humor can be difficult for some autistic students to understand and you might find yourself having to explain it sometimes. In my family, when somebody tells a joke, we all laugh, and then 30 seconds later my sister laughs because she finally got the joke, and then we all laugh again. You might find that your classroom is a bit like that.

Autistic teenagers are like all teenagers, and so sleeping in can be an issue. Some autistic students are not able to understand that, if they miss a few days in a row because they were tired, they will have more work to do when they return. Explaining what we might think are logical consequences can be very helpful for some autistic students; for example, if you put grasshoppers in your pockets and forget about them, your mother might find dead grasshoppers in the wash, and she might not like that.

Sometimes autistic students don't realize people are waiting for an answer from them. Ronca tells of when he can see his students' lips moving while they are trying to process instructions. Other teachers may think students are defying the teacher by not doing what they were asked to do, but Ronca realizes the students just don't know that they should tell the teacher they don't understand or need more time.

Some autistic students can be oblivious to others or have no social filter. Instead of saying too little, these students say too much. They seem to be rude but really, they are just being honest. Cook says this can be a real advantage because we are privy to really important thoughts that most people keep on the inside. I have had students tell me that my hair did not look good, and I had to agree that I was not having a good hair day. It's important not to react negatively to the comments—remember, offence cannot be given, it can only be taken. Don't take it. Take the information instead and use it. You might have to limit a student to four questions per period if they don't understand that other students have questions too. Or you could have to explain that the water table is for playing and not for washing shoes, as Katy Hornsby's son found out. As we get to know our autistic students, we can help them understand social norms and why they can be important. We can help them understand how their actions affect others. And then we can go home and laugh, because truthfully, I do look a bit like Peppermint Patty! (See my picture on the back of the book.)

My Clothes Are Too Itchy

Schiller's male high-school student loved her hair clips. Every day he would play with them. Schiller realized that he was doing this when he felt frustrated. Playing with the clips prevented him from having outbursts and helped him get his work done. So she spent a fortune on hair clips at the dollar store that year. This is an example of the extraordinary sensory perception that many autistic students experience. One part of getting to know our autistic students is finding out if they have unusual sensory perceptions, as this will help us help them to learn and have a good school experience. Grandin (2013, p. 71) explains that about nine out of ten people on the autism spectrum have one or more sensory disorders. She continues,

What if you're receiving the same sensory information as everyone else, but your brain is interpreting it differently? Then your experience of the world around you will be radically different from everyone else's, maybe even painfully so. In that case, you would literally be living in an alternate reality—an alternate *sensory* reality. (2013, p. 70)

Some autistic students might experience physical touch to be like fire, or the sound of a chaotic classroom could trigger auditory hallucinations, as is the case with Bailey Mandic, a young autistic man. This sensory perception makes it extremely difficult to adequately experience the outside world in order to understand it, to tolerate the environment, and then to live a social, constructive life.

Seeing

Robison relates,

> To this day, when I speak, I find visual input to be distracting. When I was younger, if I saw something interesting I might begin to watch it and stop speaking entirely. As a grown-up, I don't usually come to a complete stop, but I may still pause if something catches my eye. That's why I usually look somewhere neutral—at the ground or off into the distance—when I'm talking to someone. (2007, p. 3)

Many people are able to ignore visual distractions; Robison finds them overpowering, even as an adult. Some autistic students are not able to wear stripes, polka-dots, or patterns. Others are overwhelmed when there is too much color or too much sunlight. Similar to some people with dyslexia, when some autistic students are reading, the words on the page are wiggly.

If students are young or minimally verbal, we might not know that they are having sensory issues with seeing. Some signs of this can include them flicking fingers near their eyes, looking out of the corner of their eye when reading, having difficulty getting on or off escalators, acting blind in new places, being averse to rapid movement, or seeing print wiggling when reading (Grandin, 2013, p. 95).

If students say they are experiencing discomfort with their vision or if we notice that they are having difficulties—perhaps behavior difficulties—and that they are exhibiting some of the aforementioned behaviors that demonstrate sensory issues with sight, there are a few strategies we can try to help them feel more comfortable. As mentioned in the section on preparing your classroom (page 17), it is good to have minimal wall covering and minimal harsh lighting in the classroom. Students might want to wear a hat and/or sunglasses in class. For students who see print wiggling on the page, using pastel-colored paper might help. Some people find blue tinted glasses can help. On the computer, use various colored backgrounds. Finally, Ngui recounted that if her autistic son couldn't see something, it didn't exist. Therefore, when she was potty training, she left a potty in every room. Hopefully this won't be your exact experience—instead you can apply the idea by having pencils available in many locations throughout the room instead of keeping them only in the desk.

Hearing

Lea taught music to a developmental disabilities class one year. In it, she had two exceptionally talented drummers, and also students who were sensitive to noise.

Extraordinary sensory perceptions manifest in seeing, hearing, touching, tasting, smelling, and a combination of senses, and can result in overstimulation and understimulation.

In her class, she found the sweet spot was to do the drumming in short spurts on hand drums, not allowing anyone to bash the drums with sticks. Your classroom may need a different solution. I remember one year I had to hide the tambourines in my music classroom, as certain students loved them and others found the sound they made a bit too much (in *skillful* hands, they can be quite good). In fact, two studies found noise sensitivity to be the main problem encountered by autistic people (Krieger et al., 2018, p. 15). In these studies, autistic adolescents preferred calmer spaces in schools, such as libraries.

Again, if you have young students or minimally verbal students, they might not be able to tell you that they are sensitive to noise—in fact, it is possible they themselves don't know it. Some signs that students are sensitive to noise include appearing deaf, not being able to hear when there is background noise, difficulty hearing hard consonants, covering ears or having a sensory correction around loud sounds, ears hurting from certain sounds, hearing shutting off or changing volume, noises sounding like a bad mobile phone connection, and difficulty finding the source of a sound (Grandin, 2013, p. 96). I received custom-made ear plugs from my board of education when I taught music because the noise level in band classrooms was over the legal limit. Although they did not look cool—they were bright orange—those earplugs were very comfortable. They could be something we want to recommend to our autistic students with hearing sensitivities and their parents.

Of course, many teachers already have noise-cancelling earphones in their classrooms for students to use for working, for going to assemblies, or during a fire drill. Grandin (2013, p. 97) suggests wearing ear plugs only half the time so that students don't become even more sensitive to sound. It might also help to record the sounds that hurt a child's ears and play them back at a reduced volume, slowly increasing the volume. Another strategy is for students to be able to initiate the sound that bothers them; e.g. starting the buzzer on the scoreboard or turning on the vacuum cleaner. If a student is speaking too quietly or too loudly, show them their volume on the voice memo app on your phone and have them practice speaking at a normal volume. It might be a good idea to allow sound-sensitive students to come into the class five minutes before everyone else and leave five minutes after everyone else in order to avoid a noisy hallway. Finally, you might need to lower your volume or speak more slowly in order for autistic students with sound sensitivity to be able to hear and understand that we are telling them there is no tooth fairy (sorry …).

Touch

Meloche remarks that, in her experience, some autistic young people do not like to wear jeans because they experience them as tight and itchy. The same thing goes for underpants. Some autistic students prefer pajama bottoms because they are soft and comfortable. Meloche comments that this has caused problems for some young men going through puberty, as everyone can see when they have an erection. Clothes and tags can be so bothersome that students undress—anywhere. Other students might not want to wear deodorant or take showers because they don't like how it feels. Some students don't want to go outside when it is too cold or too hot, or they might not like the feeling of holding a pencil. It is common for autistic students to not like being touched, or even being close to another person; but others hug everyone. In fact, Grandin's mother didn't hug her because she thought that's what Grandin wanted. The problem wasn't that

A reminder that, in an effort to use more positive terminology in this book, sensory correction is used instead of *meltdown* (as recommended by Lovering Spencer).

Grandin didn't want a hug; it was that a hug "shorted out" her nervous system (2013, p. 8).

Sometimes, as a teacher, you have to have uncomfortable conversations with your autistic students. In this case, it is good to enlist the help of the parents, if possible. If not, it might help to have another teacher with you—especially one of the same gender as the student. No, this wasn't in your job description; however, if you do not have the difficult conversations, the issue will continue in your class. Pajama bottoms are okay only with a long coat over top.

For students who are too young to be very self-aware or who are unable to communicate their sensory difficulties, there are ways to ascertain if they are having tactile sensory issues. They might pull away from hugs or touch, or have a sensory correction when hugged or touched. They might take off their clothes or only wear certain articles, or they might not wear certain materials or textures. These students could seek deep pressure and want tight bear hugs, weighted blankets, or to get underneath heavy things (Grandin, 2013, p. 97). If you notice your students displaying some of these symptoms, you might want to have an explicit conversation with them, pointing out that they seem to be having trouble with tactile sensory issues and asking them if that is the case. You might use some of these strategies:

- "Wait—WHAT? Go back to the students undressing!" is probably what you are thinking right now. So let's talk about how to deal with that, because it can happen with student of any age. Students can go to the bathroom and turn their clothes inside out. This often solves the problem, as the itchy tag or seam is now on the outside. Ask the student's parents to wash all new clothes several times with fabric softener before their child wears them. Otherwise, you might want to keep some jogging pants and T-shirts in your classroom if you know your autistic student deals with this issue.
- For students who don't like to be touched, it is merely a matter of informing everyone of this fact. For students who love hugs, their parents might be able to send in a weighted blanket or a weighted vest for their child to wear when they need it.
- For students who do not want to go outside when it is cold or hot, arrange for them to go to the office or library with a book. You might have to explain to the administration or librarian that this is part of autism and not a behavioral matter.
- Lovering Spencer allows his students to wear a toque (the Canadian word for a knitted winter hat) or chew gum or give a hug to a friend when they are in distress because it helps them remain calm. Hornsby relates the story of a teacher who wanted to allow an autistic student to use a fidget toy but did not want to single out the student. Consequently, the teacher said they were going to test new things in the classroom and would pick one student to test the fidget toy. They pulled a name out of a hat and, lo and behold, it was the autistic student, who was allowed to feel good about using the fidget toy and did not feel centred out or different.

Smelling and Tasting

Hornsby says that her son would try to eat wooden toys and wicker baskets. Anything with a new texture, he would bite, lick, and feel. Some students love the smell of feces. Other students are like a pregnant woman, finding that everything has a strong, unpleasant smell. And of course, we all know children who are picky eaters and will only eat two foods; potatoes and rice, for example. Boiled potatoes, oven-roasted potatoes, mashed potatoes (oh, no, not those—they don't like the texture), scalloped potatoes, and, of course, McDonald's french fries. Some students might cry when they are too hungry. For some students, these smells and tastes can stop them from being able to concentrate and do work, as can the desire to smell and eat specific things.

Identifying these students is often easier than spotting other sensory issues because they are always eating or smelling a specific thing, or they will not eat or smell a specific thing. The only difficult part might be identifying which smell causes a student to have difficulty.

Grandin (2013, p. 98) says that the answer to these sensory issues is simple: if you don't like it, don't eat it or smell it. Or if a student is attracted to a particular strong (read bad) smell, you can try to substitute it with other strong smells; e.g. peppermint. Provide a small container with that smell so that they can open the container and smell it; the container prevents others from having to smell it. If a student is averse to a smell that cannot be avoided, nose plugs can be bought at sporting goods stores in the swimming section.

Unidentified or Combined Sensory Issues

When Hornsby's middle son was in a mainstream class in Junior Kindergarten, he was overwhelmed by the sounds and lights. In the end, he moved into a smaller class of only five students to help mitigate some of those issues. Sometimes it is difficult to determine what exactly is overloading a child's sensory system; sometimes it can be a combination of things. Mastrangelo (2009 p. 39) confirms this:

> Children with ASD can be easily overloaded by sensory stimuli (e.g., fluorescent lights, loud voices, etc.); give careful consideration to the classroom set-up, including seat assignments.

Mastrangelo recommends not only that the classroom be set up to take into account a combination of sensory issues, but also the teacher's demeanor be taken into account. In order to do this, she recommends using the acronym SMARTEST (Mastrangelo, Chiefs of Ontario Conference, 2019):

> **S**implify the language you use
> **M**ovement: slow down your actions
> **A**ffect: match the child's affect
> **R**eflect the child's emotional intent
> **T**one of voice: modulate for the situation
> **E**yes and ears: listen with both
> **S**top and wait for the child to initiate
> **T**ogether: join the child in their intent

Many of these steps include moderating the sensory input from the teacher that the child experiences. It focuses on our being slow, calm, and quieter than we may otherwise be. This increases the chance of a good sensory experience for the child, and a much nicer day for the teacher too! In fact, one spring I had been quieter than usual as a teacher. I found that I could sing higher notes at the end of the school year! My opera concert dates TBA.

When you do not know what is causing sensory corrections in a student, you might need to put on your detective hat and investigate a bit (cue Inspector Gadget music). Is the student having a difficult time at the same time of the day? In certain rooms? Around certain objects or people? It can help to keep track of when these crises occur and what happened just beforehand. Many teachers have been able to figure out at least part of the difficulty and help students avoid or overcome the sensory issues they were having. At other times, you will not be able to figure out the difficulty and will simply have to do your best to calm the student with things you know help them to relax. Often simply going for a walk with an educational assistant will help a student calm down.

There's Too Much or Too Little Going On

One mother was glad that the school had a sensory room where her son could do work. Unfortunately, after a while, he was told he should return to the classroom to do work, even though it was noisy. He was overstimulated in the classroom and unable to do the work; in the sensory room, it was quieter and he got more work done. In the end, he moved to a different school where there was more understanding.

Overstimulation

There are many good mindfulness books, including *Fostering Mindfulness* by Shelley Murphy.

Grandin (2013, p. 83) explains that when students are overstimulated, they can be over-responsive or under-responsive; they might turn off or they might act out. They might pretend to sleep on their desk or they might jump on their desk. It might look like they need more stimulation but, in reality, the world is overwhelming them and they turn off. So when a student isn't responding, it could be that they need some stimulation, or it could be that they need a break. It will take a bit of trial and error at the beginning of the year as you get to know our students. If a student is unresponsive, you could try more stimulation, only to find the student was overstimulated, and they have a sensory correction. Live and learn—probably a lesson you won't forget! Next, try reducing the stimulation. Lovering Spencer sends his students on errands so that they can walk down a quiet hallway, away from the noise of the classroom.

Mindfulness is a good way to help reduce stimulation, and often whole classes have a mindfulness break together. This can be as simple as deep breathing: i.e., breathe in for four seconds, hold your breath for four seconds, exhale for four seconds; repeat. Alternatively, students can go to the sensory corner or the Snoezelen room (see page 18). A supportive school environment can include the "availability of quiet areas such as school libraries, light dimmers, volume control of sound systems in public spaces, and repositioning of chairs to control space" (Krieger et al., 2018, p. 13). These can all give a break to students experiencing sensory overload.

Understimulation

It is pretty widely recognized that autistic children can get overstimulated and overwhelmed, but it is less well-known that they can also be understimulated and can need more stimulation in order to calm and regulate their system so they can learn. Hornsby makes sure that her sons have a steady sensory diet, as she has found that input to regulate their systems makes a world of difference to keep them calm. So she has them do "heavy work" before their homework: carrying bricks around for 15 minutes means that they can do homework for 30 minutes, no trouble. Although you won't have students carry bricks around at school, heavy books do just fine. You can identify students who are under-stimulated because they seek stimulation: they move toward colorful lights, or they touch everyone and everything in the classroom. (You have hand sanitizer in your room, right?) Lovering Spencer explains that having a sensory-rich program at every age is important, because many autistic students are kinesthetic learners who need to touch and smell in order to have their needs met and to learn. It is also important to make sure that these students move during recess because that is their time to recharge, to get out energy and to have their sensory needs met. If it is an indoor recess or if the students miss their recess for some reason, be sure to provide an opportunity for them to move around, otherwise you are setting them up for failure during the next class.

These are examples of ways in which to stimulate students who need more sensory input:

- allow them to have squeezy balls, soft cloths, containers of spices or something that smells nice, exercise bands on the bottom of their chairs, bouncy seats, fidget toys, boards with different textures
- allow them to spin in circles, have them press their hands together and squeeze as hard as they can, have them carry heavy books up and down the hall, and any (safe) physical exercise.

These exercises can help students receive the sensory input they need in order to focus on their schoolwork. Lovering Spencer had a small exercise trampoline in his classroom. He says it was only for the students…

Lesson Plan: Getting to Know Your Students

The purpose of this lesson plan is to start to get to know your students and to allow them a chance to get to know each other.

This is a great activity to do on the first day of school. Alternatively, if your autistic student is joining your class part-way through the year, it can be done on the day they join the class (or perhaps within the first week, depending on how things go).

I Like… Activity

1. Have students fill out the I Like… activity sheet on pages 38–39.
2. Direct students to try to find other students who have the same likes as theirs, and have those students write their name in the blank space provided.

I Like… Art Activity

1. Have students pick four things that they like from the I Like… activity sheet and draw a picture in each box of the I Like… Art Sheet on page 40.
2. If there is time, have students present their artwork and explain a little bit about it and about what they like.

Getting to Know Autistic Students: Checklist

Treating Students as Individuals
- ☐ Don't stereotype your autistic students.
- ☐ Don't jump right in and try to ask questions or make your students do something.
- ☐ Sit back and observe your students.
- ☐ Watch for a different presentation of autism in girls; e.g., mental-health issues alongside mild or masked autism.
- ☐ Talk to your students and their parents and look in their student record to find out if your students have any other diagnoses besides autism; e.g., ODD, ADHD, gifted, epilepsy.
- ☐ Talk with students one-on-one to build mutual trust.
- ☐ Look into their talents, interests, and quirks.
- ☐ Ascertain if challenging behavior is due to autism or is simply typical behavior.
- ☐ Be ready to use different strategies for each child.
- ☐ Invite students to eat lunch with you.
- ☐ Ask about their interests; perhaps have a survey on the first day for the whole class.

Understanding Autistic Thinking Patterns
- ☐ Determine what kind of thinker your student is.
  - ☐ Word thinkers think in words and facts.
  - ☐ Picture thinkers think in images.
  - ☐ Pattern thinkers think in patterns, especially visual/spatial patterns.
- ☐ Remember that many autistic students have a "lawyer brain" in that their thinking is very logical and fact-based.
- ☐ Redirect your autistic students when they are stuck on a fact that they think is a mistake or inconsistent.
- ☐ Avoid the use of idioms, metaphor, sarcasm.
- ☐ Use more concrete examples and assignments than hypothetical examples.
- ☐ Be ready for honest, direct talk, with little social filter.

Addressing Sensory Issues
Sight Issues
- ☐ Have subdued lighting and minimal wall coverings in your classroom.
- ☐ If students see words as wiggly, use pastel-colored paper instead of white or have the student wear tinted sunglasses.
- ☐ Allow students to wear a hat and sunglasses in class.

Hearing Issues
- ☐ Offer noise-cancelling headphones in your classroom.
- ☐ Allow students control over the noise; e.g., let them push the buzzer to end the basketball game.
- ☐ Allow students to come to class and leave class 5 minutes early to avoid noisy hallways.

Touch Issues
- ☐ When clothes are itchy, allow students to go to the bathroom to turn them inside out and have extra soft clothes on hand.
- ☐ Let students go to the library or office for recess if they are sensitive to extreme cold or heat.
- ☐ Allow students to use fidget toys, bouncy seats, weighted vests, etc.

Smell and Taste Issues
- ☐ Some autistic students will avoid or really enjoy certain smells and tastes; as much as possible, allow them to do this.
- ☐ Try to substitute another strong smell (e.g., peppermint) if a student likes an offensive smell (e.g., rotten eggs, feces).

Unidentified or Combined Sensory Issues
- ☐ Use the acronym SMARTEST to monitor your demeanor (see page 34).
- ☐ Try to figure out what is setting off sensory corrections by recording when they occur and what happened just beforehand.
- ☐ If you are unable to ascertain the cause, help the student calm down.

Overstimulation
- ☐ Let students go to the sensory corner or Snoezelen room to do work.
- ☐ Send students to other quiet areas, including the library or study hall.
- ☐ Send students on errands so they can get away from the noisy classroom.
- ☐ Use mindfulness activities, including breathing exercises.

Understimulation
- ☐ Have students do "heavy work" before sitting to do class work; e.g., carry heavy books up and down the hall.
- ☐ Have a sensory-rich program for every age, because many students are kinesthetic learners.
- ☐ Make sure students get exercise at recess, even if it is an indoor recess.
- ☐ Use squeezy balls, soft cloths, containers of spices or something that smells nice, exercise bands on the bottom of their chairs, bouncy seats, fidget toys, boards with different textures; allow them to spin, have them press their hands together and squeeze as hard as they can.

Pembroke Publishers ©2021 *What's the Difference?* by Amanda Yuill ISBN 978-1-55138-348-4

I Like...

Circle as many of the options as you like—you do not have to choose only one. When you are done, find someone who likes the same thing as you and ask them to write their name in the blank. You cannot have the same person write their name more than once on your sheet. You must find a different person for each question.

1. What kind of movies do you like?
   Comedy
   Action/Adventure
   Romance
   Drama
   Documentary
   Science Fiction
   My favorite movie is _____

   Name of the person who likes the same movies as me: _____

2. What kind of food do you like?
   Sweet
   Salty
   Savory
   Bitter
   Sour
   My favorite food is _____

   Name of the person who likes the same foods as me: _____

3. What kind of drinks do you like?
   Pop
   Hot drinks
   Juice
   Water
   Milk
   My favorite drink is _____

   Name of the person who likes the same drink as me: _____

4. What kind of sports do you like?
   Ball sports
   Strength and Combat sports (e.g. wrestling)
   Track and Field/Endurance sports
   Water/Snow/Ice sports
   My favorite sport is_____

   Name of the person who likes the same sports as me: _____

5. What kind of pets do you like?
   Dogs
   Cats
   Rodents; e.g. hamsters, mice
   Fish
   Other: _____

   My favorite pets are _____

   Name of the person who likes the same pets as me:_____

Pembroke Publishers ©2021 *What's the Difference?* by Amanda Yuill ISBN 978-1-55138-348-4

I Like... (cont'd)

6. What kind of games do you like?
   Card games
   Word games
   Strategy games; e.g. chess
   Games of chance; e.g. Snakes and Ladders

   Other: _____

   My favorite game is _____

   Name of the person who likes the same games as me: _____

7. What kind of books do you like?
   Mystery
   Comedy
   Drama
   Romance
   Science Fiction/Fantasy
   Manga/Cartoon

   Other: _____

   My favorite book is _____

   Name of the person who likes the same books as me: _____

8. What is your favorite way to travel?
   Car
   Train
   Airplane
   Boat
   Other: _____

   My favorite way to travel is _____

   Name of the person who likes the same way to travel as me: _____

9. What kind of vacations do you like?
   Staying at home
   Cottage
   Beach
   Cruise
   Another Country

   Other: _____

   My favorite place to go on vacation is _____

   Name of the person who likes the same vacations as me: _____

10. What school subjects do you like?
    Math
    Language
    Science
    Physical Education
    Art
    Music
    Other: _____

    My favorite subject is _____

    Name of the person who likes the same subjects as me: _____

Pembroke Publishers ©2021 *What's the Difference?* by Amanda Yuill ISBN 978-1-55138-348-4

I Like… Art Sheet

3

Helping Autistic Students do Schoolwork

See page 54 for a checklist for Helping Autistic Students Do Schoolwork.

I taught an autistic boy in Grade 3 who loved science and went to science camp in the summer. He also performed experiments in my classroom. One time he put a bead in his ear to see what would happen (even though I thought I had taken all the beads away from him earlier, when I found him putting them in his nose). He found out he couldn't hear very well and that the doctor at the hospital had to use a tool to get it out. He was fascinated. Then he told his mother that someone threw the bead onto the floor, it bounced up and got caught in his ear. Some of your autistic students will love school (and science) and will not need a lot of help understanding your lessons and getting their work done. Others will need more help.

We want to make sure that our students are understanding what we are teaching. This might call for modifying or chunking the work. For some students, modifying or chunking the work is similar to allowing a student with severe cerebral palsy to use a wheelchair. Some students might come to school with a computer or a tablet or other assistive technology. Yes, this does mean that you will have to know how to work their technology (I know you can do it!). The goal is not only for students to learn, but also for them to work independently. Sometimes long-distance or online learning might be necessary. In these cases, we want to make sure that the students' technology is not bothering them or preventing them from learning. You know how you don't like to listen to yourself once you've been recorded? Most people are like that.

Unlocking the Walls

At first, we cannot see how some autistic students learn and so some people assume they cannot learn. Hucklebridge explains that it is like they are behind four castle walls. The key, she says, is to decode what's behind the walls, to unlock the walls to see how these students learn. Schiller expressed the same idea about her students:

I find it challenging to be able to figure out where they are at and what they need. I'm up for the challenge—it's like being a scientist. I'm going to discover something and I'm going to be able to empower this person to have the best life they can, to discover what their talents are and how they can use them. Anyone can take that approach—it is exciting and interesting. You're treading on unknown territory with each and every one of them. That's a good way to look at it.

The mission, should you choose to accept it (cue the *Mission Impossible* theme music), is to find the keys to unlock the way each child learns.

Follow the IEP

When you are looking to modify your program for an autistic student, the first place to look is in their Individual Education Plan (IEP), which lists modifications needed. Tom says that when he was in high school, he would dictate some of his work and the teachers would write it down; he found this very helpful. Other teachers gave him digital copies of the work. These are common modifications found on an IEP.

Even when an IEP is followed, I have found that students can regress (especially at first, with a new teacher) and so you might need to make the lesson simpler for the student to have success. A good rule of thumb is to aim for the student to have success 80% of the time. Ronca points out that often there are three expectations for a subject on an IEP; however, only one is reported on the report card. For example, for Social Studies, an IEP could list these three expectations:

1) identify various physical regions in Canada;
2) identify Canada's provinces and territories and their capital cities;
3) demonstrate an understanding of cardinal directions (north, east, south, west).

However, the only expectation reported on the report card might be *2) identify Canada's provinces and territories and their capital cities.* To simplify the curriculum expectations on the IEP further, a five-minute conversation might cover one of the expectations adequately for autistic students. For example, a five-minute conversation about the physical regions in Canada would cover that curriculum expectation and be enjoyable and understandable for students. Ronca suggests asking students to name one province and one capital, and to make it a game (be sure not to pick St. John, or is it St. John's—that's confusing!). The goal is to cover the curriculum so that the students can learn and so that they can enjoy learning.

If you are unable to find a good balance with the IEP, Sari Lansimaki, a former educator, encourages teachers to ask someone for help: perhaps the student's previous teacher or the Special Education Resource Teacher (SERT). It's important to use positive language on the IEP and to make sure to follow it. When a student starts to improve, don't take away the modifications without discussing it with them first. That's sort of like taking away the battery pack from an electric wheelchair. Pushing an electric wheelchair is not fun, and the IEP is there to help the teacher and the child. So for goodness' sake, let's use it!

Individualized Modifications

In the article, "How to Teach Autistic Pupils…By Autistic Pupils" Craig Goodall (2020) tells the story of an autistic student:

> Dan, aged 11, spoke of how a visual schedule was imposed on him. This is a textbook autism strategy, often discussed during autism teacher-training events. But this only served to frustrate him, as he neither wanted nor needed it.

As teachers, we need to find a modification that actually helps the student.

- Hancock wore pants and a sweatshirt to high-school gym class, as he did not feel comfortable in front of 50 students in shorts (I can understand that—those shorts are often short shorts!). He got marked down because of that. The fact that Hancock did not change into his shorts despite the lower mark indicates to me that a modification was needed.
- Meloche's son would not redo work. He would do a whole new assignment on the same topic, but he would not go over his work to correct it because he thought it was already correct.

Often, a student needing a modification can look like stubbornness or bad behavior. In fact, it is often part of the autism. We need to be careful not to punish students for their autism. Lovering Spencer says the best modifications allow students to be in Vygotsky's Zone of Proximal Development, where the student is working on a skill that they are able to do with guidance (not a skill they are unable to do, and not a skill they can do on their own). This will push them to the next step. It can also help to give the student their choice of modification. For example, at the end of a novel study, you can give the student a choice of having you scribe for them, using voice typing, or writing half a page instead of a full page. When we allow students to use modifications, we are often surprised by the level of the work presented—even if they are not in shorts.

Location

Maybe our autistic students can't go anywhere in the world to work, but perhaps there are a few places in the school they can go to work. Lothian taught a high-school student who would go to class for ten to fifteen minutes and then go back to his little cubby in the resource room or to the sensory room to do his work. Welker confirms that her son also liked to work in the resource room. If possible, it is good to have two or three quiet places where an autistic student can go to work, even if they simply work in the sensory corner in your classroom with a noise-cancelling headset. As long as you have arranged this with the librarian, resource teacher, etc., and you know where your student is, this is an easy modification that can make the world of difference.

Routine

When I was a substitute teacher, I went into a Kindergarten class where the students thought I was not a very good teacher because I did not know that I was supposed to do the calendar after the national anthem, not before. They had a routine they liked and I was messing it up! It is often this way for autistic students: they have a routine and they like the predictability. Lothian agrees that having a program and going through the routine every day helps her students focus. Meloche suggests having a very detailed syllabus for high-school courses so that autistic students know what is coming next. Routine helps reduce anxiety, helps students get their schoolwork done, and makes you look like a great teacher, in their eyes. Of course, I'm sure you are a great teacher in anyone's eyes!

Time

Have you ever been on a school bus without a teacher? I mean, looking back to when you weren't a teacher. I have. I remember the bus driver yelling at us (a Grade 8 class on the way to shop class at another school) and then going back to the school to say he would not take us because we were too loud and obnoxious. The bus ride to school in the morning can be stressful. Some of the students might even be harnessed in. So for the first 15 minutes of class, after they ride the school bus, Ronca allows his students to flop on the couch, read a book, or do nothing. If they read out loud, he does not ask them to read in their head. He just allows them to relax in their own way. Sometimes students, especially younger students, need time to sleep. Lea taught a boy who would fall asleep last period on the gym bench. She felt he needed it, so she let him sleep. Students might need time to get something to eat. It may be that, in order to get work done, some students just need to sit there for five minutes to process. I need that too, sometimes, along with a snack!

Be Specific

Kyriakides' six-year-old nephew, who has mild autism, asked if he could wash his hands. Kyriakides jokingly said, "Yes, you can use my water." He put his hands in her glass of water to wash his hands. Some autistic students are very literal. It is best to be as specific as possible, even about things that seem to be self-explanatory. For example, you might have to go over how to raise your hand to ask a question in class, even when students are older. You might have to go over raising a hand to ask a question, and then waiting for the teacher to call your name before asking the question. Kyriakides's nephew had a difficult time with one assignment because he thought you had to write exactly three lines to answer every question because there were three lines under each question. He didn't realize that you could write two lines, or that you could put an arrow to show the rest of the answer was on the back of the page. This is why it is a good idea to check in on your autistic students once in a while as they are working to make sure there is no misunderstanding. Of course, they will think there is no misunderstanding, as they did *exactly* what you said to do.

Re-explain/Illustrate/Describe

I remember not understanding how to tell time. I was in Grade 2 and everyone else was finished their worksheet and I could not figure it out. Why were there fractions with time; e.g., quarter to two? I'm sure my teacher explained it to me over and over again until I understood in Grade 4—okay, maybe Grade 3—but definitely not in Grade 2. Sometimes autistic students just need you to explain again. And explain in the exact same words because they are still processing what we said and, if we change our words, they will have to start processing again. Sometimes, they need you to explain again in different words. Yano says that teachers needed patience with him when he was in school because he needed them to explain in a few different ways, using different words. Because he has Asperger syndrome, the teachers thought he should understand, and often he did. At times, however, he honestly needed more help. More than simply using different words, use illustrations or manipulatives to help explain, and explain again. Rathee suggests using a bigger font and colorful pictures to help attract students to the work. If they don't understand, she suggests showing a bit of a movie or some pictures on the computer to help. To this day, I prefer digital clocks and, as I was born in the last millennium, I find a bigger font does help!

Movement

In my class, I like to have dance breaks. The younger children pop right up and get to dancing. The older students come around slowly, but usually, by the end of the year, they are also popping right up and dancing too! We all need a movement break once in a while. This can be especially true for autistic students, who need the sensory input. After they move around for a while, they will be able to do more work. April Coombs's son needed to fiddle while he listened, so his teacher allowed him to sit at his desk during circle time; she provided him with a picture and asked him to write about it, as she knew he liked to write. It might have looked like he was not participating in circle time, yet he knew what was going on when asked.

If you want students to do their work, you might need to provide stress balls, fidget toys, balloon seats, and the opportunity to go for a walk. Rathee suggests telling students they can go for a five-minute walk and giving them the boundaries of where they can go. These breaks not only help students do work, they can also reduce anxiety. Dance breaks help reduce anxiety only if you know you are not a bad dancer. And you are not a bad dancer. There are dancers and there are good dancers but there are no bad dancers—no, that's a lie! (Stop arguing with me about this in your mind where I'm not there to argue back. Just accept that I'm right!)

Feeling Safe

You know the dream where you are naked at work? Do you remember the feeling of fear? Fear and anxiety stop students from learning. Grandin (Leading Edge Seminars, 2020) says that some pupils are terrified to make a mistake. So she teaches them to make a paper snowflake, which, she asserts, many have not done. Because it is only paper, if they make a mistake, it is not a big deal. She wants them to know it's okay to make mistakes. You can foster this atmosphere in your classrooms by making it safe to make mistakes and, therefore, safe to learn. When he was in school, Hancock did not like to be in front of the class doing presentations or forced into a group with someone he didn't like. He preferred to be given alternative ways to demonstrate his learning.

Trying to find their own partner can cause some autistic students anxiety, and so it is sometimes better to assign partners. One of my autistic students asked if I could assign partners in gym class as nobody wanted to be his partner ☹. As we get to know our students, we can partner them with friends or allow them to choose, whichever makes it safer for them to learn. We want to help students feel that the classroom is a safe environment in which to learn and do schoolwork, because nobody likes the feeling of being embarrassed and vulnerable—even if it is just a dream.

Chunking

No, chunking is not some new slang for throwing up! Chunking is the process of breaking work down into smaller pieces. As a U.S. Army general said, "When eating an elephant, take one bite at a time." For some autistic children, every assignment is like eating an elephant—huge and overwhelming. Therefore, instead of giving them the whole assignment the week before it is due, break it down into smaller chunks and give them one part of the assignment to do each day. For example, the first day, the students could go to the library and choose two books on the subject. The second day, they could make jot notes from the two books. The third day, they could write two paragraphs using their jot notes. The fourth day, they could edit the paper with a friend. The fifth day, they could write out their good copy. Even assignments that are due in one period can be chunked. Meloche's daughter works best when her work is chunked. She needs to know just the next thing—not everything.

Everything About Penguins

I remember meeting a young autistic girl in a computer class I was teaching. The educational assistants advised me to allow her to watch baking videos when she was done with her work. I would also watch them with her, and I started to get hooked. I thought, "I'm supposed to be influencing her, not the other way around!" Now, I love Chef John, who has the *Food Wishes* YouTube channel. I especially recommend watching his Baked Stuffed Brie video.

As teachers, we are very familiar with using students' interests as incentives to help them finish their schoolwork. This can backfire, however, as some students rarely finish their work and therefore rarely, if ever, get the incentive. In *Autism and Behaviorism*, Kohn observes that some therapists "are trained to find out what your child loves most and hold it [for] ransom." Obviously, as teachers, we don't want to withhold a child's passion from them—we want to incorporate it into our teaching.

As a vice-principal, Lea encourages her teachers to find something that perks up their students, something that gets their mojo going. She reassures her teachers that we can't always follow the curriculum, that sometimes we have to go with whatever grabs the students' interest. Grandin (2013, p. 185) encourages teachers to expand on the student's interest:

> If he's drawing pictures of racecars all the time, ask him to draw the racetrack too. Then ask him to draw the streets and buildings around the racetrack. If he can do that, then we've taken his weakness (obsessional thinking about an object) and turned it into a strength (a way to understand the relationship between something as simple as a racecar and the rest of society).

Kluth & Schwarz (2008, p. 74) are of the same mind, and give the example of a student who loves spiders. They recommend asking the student to make a world map that includes which species of spider can be found in each country to ensure that geography is being learned. Perhaps it will help you get over your fear of spiders as a bonus. Oh, it's your students, and not you, who are afraid of spiders? Sorry, my mistake. For the younger student who loves Mickey Mouse, simply adding a sticker to a worksheet can increase her interest and motivation. Boff used SpongeBob and trains to encourage one of her students to count, learn colors, and explore positional relationships (e.g., under, over). Joel Smith explains:

> I've been asked what it feels like to be immersed in an obsession. It is absolutely wonderful! Time seems to stop, and nothing could bother me while I'm pursuing my "obsession". It doesn't drain me, but it energizes me. I wouldn't give up these "obsessions" for anything. (Kluth and Schwarz, 2008, p. 118)

This is what we want for our students, to be energized by the learning.

Sometimes, as teachers, we are reluctant to include a student's interests in our lessons, concerned that the student will be interested in only that one thing and not anything else. It could be your student's passion goes against cultural norms. (This might remind some of us of people we live with: why is it not okay to be passionate about trains or computers, but it is okay to be passionate about hockey or fashion?) This is where your creativity as a teacher comes into play. If you can see your students' interests as passions instead of obsessions, they can be potential tools to help your students be calmer and more successful as they learn. There are many benefits to using your students' passions in your lessons.

Winter-Messiers (2007) found that autistic people changed when someone encouraged them to talk about their interests:

> She noticed… that the intelligibility of the participants increased markedly, as did the sophistication of their use of vocabulary, world order, and syntax… improvement in body language and a decrease in distraction and repetitive behaviors. (p. 140)

In fact, it is especially helpful in high school to discuss how a student's passion could lead to a career. It is possible to look at a passion and see it as calming, motivating, and even inspiring. All the same, sometimes an interest may not have a purpose besides bringing joy to the student. And that is okay.

But I Don't Need a Calculator

One high-school student was developing his own computer coding language at home. He had a difficult time understanding why he had to do assignments in his computer science class that he could do in five minutes. They were so easy for him, he didn't understand why he had to hand them in. The trick for this student was to set and maintain a routine. Although this can be difficult, it can help students do non-preferred tasks and not get lost in what they love to do, to the detriment of the rest of their lives (including combing their hair, sometimes).

Many autistic people have areas of strength and some have autistic genius. Grandin (2013, p. 142) tells the story of Daniel Tammet, who recited 22,514 digits of pi in five hours in 2004 as a fundraiser for research for epilepsy. George and Charles Finn were able to tell you the day of the week for any date 40,000 years in the past or future (Silberman, 2015, p. 316). Focusing on a student's strengths and allowing them to use their strengths in the classroom is important for their self-esteem. Like many people with Asperger's, Robison grew up thinking there was something wrong with him. Through his experiences as an adult, including inventing and implementing special effects for shows for the heavy metal band KISS, he came to realize,

> I'm not defective. In fact, in recent years I have started to see that we Aspergians are *better* than normal! And now it seems as though scientists agree: Recent articles suggest that a touch of Asperger's is an essential part of much creative genius. (Robison, 2007, p. 240)

In fact, Asperger himself agreed, saying, "It seems that for success in science and art, a dash of autism is essential" (cited in Silberman, 2015, p. 103).

In 2007, Michelle Dawson found that all previous autism research had focused on the weaknesses of autism and so she decided to research the strengths. She found that when intelligence was tested with nonverbal methods, autistic children and adults scored in the normal range (Grandin, 2013, p. 117). Therefore, in the classroom, if we are having difficulty helping a student understand an idea, it might help to try to explain using our student's strengths; for example, using pictures or some other nonverbal means. If you are doing a novel study with intermediate students whose strength is art, Boff suggests asking students to draw the meaning of a book or of their favorite part of the book instead of having them write it. On a math test, it might not be necessary for students to show all their work and all the steps they used to get the answers. They might have just known the answer because math is one of their strengths. The key is to focus on the students' strengths and use them, instead of focusing on their weaknesses. I know I appreciate it when people focus on my strengths—like guessing other people's drawings in Pictionary—rather than my weaknesses—like drawing pictures in Pictionary. No, it's an elevator, not a giraffe!

There are many strengths that are often associated with autism and/or Asperger syndrome, according to Grandin (2013, p. 120), including seeing details, a detailed memory, bottom-up thinking (seeing the details before the whole or seeing the details that create the whole), creative thinking, associative thinking (when presented with a new idea, seeing other, similar pictures in their brain), music, math, and many others. Lovering Spencer recommends showing other students in the class how brilliant your autistic student is in their areas of strength and allowing them to use the autistic student as a resource in that area. Once, on a field trip, Lovering Spencer had everyone get off a streetcar because his autistic student, who had memorized all of the streetcar routes, said to—even though it seemed like a mistake. As they watched the streetcar pull away, it turned a corner instead of going straight. There are other ways we can benefit sometimes, when we look for strengths and then encourage them—especially if the strength is baking!

Pink Polka-Dot Wallpaper in My Virtual Classroom

Even though I am a pretty good typist (says me), I decided to use Google Voice Typing in Google Docs to input part of this book. I thought it might be faster and easier, and it mostly is; however, sometimes it is annoying. It doesn't always write down exactly what I said (typing out "egg sample" instead of "example"—why would I be writing about sampling eggs?). Tom divulges that, even though using a computer to write was on his IEP in high school because of his illegible handwriting (I know how you feel, Tom; people always used to tell me I would be a doctor because my handwriting was and is illegible), he found it difficult to convince his teachers to allow him to use one. Educational technology in the classroom is a great example of UDL that can be beneficial for all our students, and using a computer to help students write is just one example of this. Even if we are not using Google Docs, there is a lot of free dictation software available, and many word-processing programs now have it built in. This can be a lifesaver for the students and for teachers, too, if we do not have time to scribe for our students. You do have to add in punctuation, by saying "period" or "comma" out loud, and sometimes it mishears or starts writing down the conversation going on beside the autistic student (Hey, that's *my* pencil); however, it's still possible to get down the idea of what the student wanted to say. The main point is not that the student is able to write down their ideas (unless this is the object of the lesson). The main point is that we see what the student understood and learned from the lesson. This can be difficult to remember sometimes.

Reading and writing are two of the main uses for educational technology for autistic students. In fact, using a tablet or computer at school has revolutionized many students' ability to learn. There are a variety of websites and apps that read to students or that teach students how to read or write, including Read and Write, Starfall, Bookflix, Writing Without Tears, and many more. You might be required to sign up or even pay to use some of these (or put up with the annoying advertising—yes, I am happy with how white my teeth are, thank you). However, many boards of education have contracts with various companies so that teachers can use their services free of charge in the classroom or for educational purposes.

More than learning skills or information, technology can help prepare autistic students for new experiences that could otherwise be alarming or unsettling. Boff uses technology to prepare her students for field trips. It is possible to do a virtual tour of many museums and galleries. It is possible to use Google Maps Street View to show the front of a specific location or even what the route will look like on the way to the destination. There are many videos of students at a zoo, at a swim program, or hiking. Boff prints out pictures of every activity that will happen on the trip and goes over it with her students in the days leading up to the excursion. She has also used this method to prepare students for writing standardized tests, and it could be adopted to help prepare students for fire drills and lockdowns as well.

Technology can help make the lessons more relatable to the student's lives. Using an autistic student's strengths and interests in our lessons is much more easily done when using technology. Older or more-able students can do this for themselves. Boff tells of how, in a media unit, Grade 7 students found a website that listed the calories in fast-food breakfast sandwiches. This was interesting to them, as they often went to McDonalds and Starbucks to eat breakfast sandwiches before school, and it made the media unit more relevant to their lives. I know I usually don't order food from fast-food restaurants when I see the calories listed. I prefer ignorance when eating my desserts! If your school board is like mine, the textbooks are mostly out of date and I more often use online sources to help plan my lessons, which include a lot more use of technology than traditional textbook-and-worksheet lessons.

It is helpful to be prepared when students come to class with a laptop the school provided for them, or when parents ask us to use technology recommended by their doctors or therapists. It's a good thing. As much as possible, I recommend working with the student and the technology that comes with them. It's possible to see it as a tool to help the students learn, and not as the end of the world as we know it, like my grandmother used to say. She had a dream that computers would one day fail...

I have barely scratched the surface of the use of educational technology for autistic students. This topic could be a whole book by itself (that would be out of date by the time it was published, at the rate technology moves). I have not mentioned virtual classrooms, the use of smart phones, video software, and much, much more. The point of this section is not to give an exhaustive list of educational technology, but to give a few ideas that can easily be implemented into the classroom with very little effort on the teacher's part and that yield great results.

Please, Just Read for Five Minutes!

Working independently can be very difficult for some autistic students. Lea remembers one year when the special education teacher and librarian would come to her classroom to work with an autistic boy. He would do most of his work when they were helping him. Most of the rest of the time, when Lea was working with the whole class, he would play. He was safe and happy, and he was playing, not doing schoolwork. Ronca agrees that working independently can be difficult for some autistic students—he says that even with five specialists advising you in your classroom, at the end of the year, a student might be able to work independently for five minutes. This might not seem like much, but could provide valuable skills. So the question is, if we want to help all our students learn, and we cannot help each individually at the same time, how do we promote independent work with our autistic students?

There are many small, relatively easy techniques teachers can use to promote independent work. Of course, attitude makes a difference—Ngui taught her children to say, "I'm trying to…" instead of, "I can't…" She found that they were always saying they couldn't do something, but when she took time to address the attitude and to help change the language they were using it helped a lot. Boff encourages her students to add the word "yet" to "I can't" so that they come to realize that at some point, they will be able to achieve the goal. Hornsby adds that incentives are also helpful in promoting independent work, especially visual incentives. She found that breaking down activities into small chunks and then using positive reinforcement helped reduce the resistance to learning new things. Working with a partner can also help students maintain their focus and complete work without the teacher's constant supervision. But the choice of a mature partner is crucial. As we all know, the wrong partner can mean the modeling clay ends up in someone's hair…

One tool that can make all the difference is an Independent Activity Schedule (IAS). This is a tool that signals a child to complete a group of activities. An IAS has a set of pictures or words, each indicating a different activity. The idea is that the child looks at the first word or picture, does that activity, and then puts it away. They look at the next picture or word, do that activity, and then put it away. This continues until they have completed all of the activities on the IAS, which usually takes between five and twenty minutes. Some students take to this like a duck to water and will be working independently in no time. For some students, five minutes seems like a miracle. Good thing I believe in miracles! If a student is receiving support or therapy through the community, they might have already been taught how to use an IAS, and this skill can then be transferred to the classroom. Some organizations have therapists come into the classroom to work with the student on an IAS in the classroom.

The key to using an IAS is to start very easily and slowly. The activities have to be something the student can do on their own and something that has a specific end; e.g. put beads on a string, complete a small puzzle, paint by numbers, sort buttons, etc. It is okay to use open-ended activities if we also teach the student to use a timer and set a time for each activity. It is important that whatever signals the activity is clear. For example, make sure the picture of the puzzle does not have a picture of a computer in the background. It is also a good idea to have all of the activities easily accessible and in the same place to start—for example, in bins on a shelf near their desk. Another recommendation is to start with activities the student likes; for example, eating a snack. One picture can be of a snack and the child is to get their snack, eat it, and put away the container or garbage at the end. In fact, if the snack is the last item on the IAS, this can be the incentive for finishing it. Lays chips, anyone?

Surrey Place recommends having an IAS for all the students in your class, so your autistic student can learn by copying others. They will not feel singled out when they complete it, as it is a classroom activity everybody does. Obviously, a student needs to be able to match the picture to the activity; if they are unable to

For more information on how to set up an IAS and video examples, see https://www.surreyplace.ca/setting-up-an-ias-in-the-home/

do this, an IAS is not the tool for them. Also, it often can take a couple of months for a student to learn to use an IAS, so don't give up when they have difficulty at first. And at second, and at third. It is likely they are having difficulty with just one step, and might simply need some help or an incentive to learn that step and move onto the next one. Once a student learns how to use an IAS, you give them a choice of activities that will go on their IAS that day; for example, you pick two activities and they pick two activities. Also, worksheets or other schoolwork can be added as activities once they know how to follow an IAS.

I Don't Like Looking at Myself on the Screen

In June 2020, I was in an online meeting for a Grade 7 class. Because of COVID-19, we had been doing online classes for about three months. One of the boys in the class said, "I can't believe I'm saying this, but I'm tired of my computer and I want to come back to school!" Online or distance learning can be very difficult for students, and there are some things we can do to help our autistic students with it. First of all, having a routine is important. Making sure that you meet at the same time every day or the same time every week is really important. Then, when you teach an online lesson, it helps if you stick to the same routine every time, as much as possible. You can continue to use your visual schedule and any other visual aids you have found helpful in the classroom. If you are doing distance learning, you will need to introduce the routine and visual aids to the students in your first class or the first few classes.

Before many of you were born, sometimes TV pictures would flicker. We used to put tin foil on the antenna (yes, TVs had antennae) and point the antenna toward the window to get a better picture. We sometimes even attached coat hangers to the ends of an antenna to extend its reach; in a pinch, someone would have to stand with one arm touching the antenna and the other arm stretched toward the window (or whatever way gave the best reception), just to get a good picture. This is what it can be like for some autistic students when the Internet connection is bad. They can get distracted by the flickering picture and spend time trying to fix the picture instead of learning. Older tablets, laptops, and other equipment can also cause a flickering picture. For this reason, I recommend to parents that, if possible, they get the best Internet connection and computer they can and that they use a Local Area Network (LAN) cable to connect the computer to the Internet instead of using WiFi. Also, some students might not like being able to see themselves on the screen, so it can be helpful to have them hide the picture of themselves. Other students love the picture of themselves and are also distracted by it, making faces at themselves that all the students can see. For this reason, too, you might want to minimize their picture. These are all things that you may have to set up with the parents before the first online class, if possible—although it is not always possible.

There are many reasons you might be teaching online or distance learning classes. Students might live in a remote location; students might have a medical condition that prevents them from physically coming to school; or there might be other circumstances, ranging from a pandemic to bear sightings, the zombie apocalypse, alien invasions—really, anything is possible. When Tom was in high school, a teacher came to his house once a week due to health issues unrelated to his autism, and he worked on his own the rest of the time. He was able to do only half a course load. With this sort of situation, we can't know how much access a student will have to technology. Even if we are doing lessons online with them instead of in person, it does not mean that they will have access to a computer or the Internet when we are not teaching them (or sometimes, even when we are scheduled to teach them). For this reason, we need to have a variety of work ready for them to do, both low-tech and high-tech. It is also important to adjust expectations of how much work can be done online. Each student will have a different capacity. Sometimes we simply expect too much from our students—and from ourselves.

Lesson Plan: Getting Homework Done

The purpose of this lesson plan is to expose students to a variety of strategies to help them find one that works for them and to encourage them to do their homework.

Some students have a really difficult time getting their homework done, even if it is simply to read for 20 minutes every day. Use this lesson plan if you notice that some of your students are having difficulty consistently completing their homework.

Brainstorming Activity

1. Have students break up into groups of two to four.
2. Instruct students to brainstorm strategies to help them complete their homework when they don't feel like it.
3. Give students about 10 minutes to write down strategies
4. Come back together as a class and have each group present their ideas.

Sharing Strategies

If your students haven't mentioned these strategies, share them with your other students:

- Set a timer for five minutes. Work hard for five minutes, then take a five minute break, then work hard for five minutes. Each night, increase the amount of time you work; e.g., work for 10 minutes, take a break for five minutes. Aim for working for 20 minutes, and then taking a five-minute break.
- Put your phone on silent mode while doing homework.
- Listen to music to block out other sounds.
- Have a list of what you have to do and cross off each item as you finish it.
- Set an incentive for yourself; e.g., you can eat a piece of popcorn each time you finish a question, or play a video game when you are done the whole sheet.
- Have a study partner. You can compete to see who gets the work done fastest or help each other with difficult questions.
- Move to a different spot, a quiet spot with no distractions.
- Do the easy parts first.

Practicing Strategies

Tell students that you are going to try three of these strategies from Sharing Strategies in class. The students can use any work they have or you can assign work for this time. Be sure that everyone has at least 30 minutes of work to do.

1. Let the class know that the first strategy you are going to try is the timer method. You are going to set a timer for five minutes and they are going to work hard for five minutes and then have five minutes free time.

2. Tell students the second strategy you are going to try is to work with a study partner. They can compete or help each other, as long as they are not fooling around. Have students work with their study partner for 10 minutes. Discuss how you could have a study partner when you live far away; e.g., calling each other on the phone or video chat.

3. For the third strategy, allow students to choose one to try. Alternatively, you can combine strategies by having students move to a spot away from distractions and turning on quiet, instrumental music while they work for 10 minutes. You could also add an incentive if you choose; e.g., watching a funny YouTube video with the class when they are done.

4. Come together as a class and discuss which strategy students liked best and why. Ask if there are any other strategies students are going to try. Talk about the consequences of not finishing homework.

Helping Students Do Schoolwork: Checklist

Modifications
- ☐ Read the IEP; follow the IEP; adjust the IEP.
- ☐ Allow the student to have success 80% of the time.
- ☐ Discuss changes to the IEP with the student before changing it.
- ☐ Modify the skill so that the student can do it with guidance.
- ☐ Give students a choice of activities/modifications to demonstrate their learning.

Location
- ☐ Have 2 or 3 quiet places prepared where students are allowed to go to work if the classroom is too noisy.
- ☐ Arrange with other teachers/librarian ahead of time that your student is allowed to work with them instead of in the classroom (e.g., in the library, special education room, study hall).
- ☐ Have noise-cancelling headphones in the sensory corner in your classroom.

Routine
- ☐ Follow a daily routine.
- ☐ Have a detailed syllabus for high-school classes.

Time
- ☐ Give students free time the first 15 minutes of the day after they arrive at school.
- ☐ Give students time to eat, or even sleep, if they need it.
- ☐ Give students time to process what you have said.

Be Specific
- ☐ Be ready to explain things that seem to be self-explanatory or that most students would know without being told.
- ☐ Be specific about what you would like students to do.

Re-explain/Illustrate/Describe
- ☐ Explain a second or third time using the exact same words.
- ☐ Explain a different way the second time and another way the third time.
- ☐ Use pictures instead of words.
- ☐ Use bigger, more colorful fonts on handouts.

Movement
- ☐ Have dance breaks.
- ☐ Allow students to fidget while listening to lessons or doing work.
- ☐ Allow students to go for a walk.

Feeling Safe
- ☐ Nurture a classroom atmosphere in which it is okay to make mistakes.
- ☐ Practice making mistakes; e.g., make paper snowflakes.
- ☐ Allow students to work with a friend when working with partners.
- ☐ Allow students an alternative to speaking in front of the class in order to demonstrate their learning.

Chunking
- ☐ Break assignments down into smaller chunks instead of giving the student the whole assignment at once.

Using Students' Interests
- ☐ Incorporate students' interests into lessons, as well as using them as incentives.
- ☐ Expand on the students' interest; e.g., draw the racetrack, not just the racecar.
- ☐ See students' interests as passions and not obsessions.
- ☐ Discuss how a student's passion could lead to a career.

Working with Strengths
- ☐ Improve self-esteem by emphasizing student's strengths.
- ☐ Use nonverbal methods of communication.
- ☐ Use an autistic student's strengths as a resource for other students.

Educational Technology
- ☐ Use dictation technology when writing is difficult.
- ☐ Use software programs to read to students.
- ☐ Use technology to prepare students for field trips, fire alarms, standardized testing, etc.
- ☐ Use technology to make lessons relatable.

Working Independently
- ☐ Use the language "I'm trying to…" instead of "I can't…"
- ☐ Use incentives, chunking, and partners to make working independently easier.
- ☐ Use an IAS.

Online/Distance Learning
- ☐ Have a routine.
- ☐ Use visual aids.
- ☐ Talk to parents about having good equipment and a good Internet connection, about using a cable to connect to the Internet.
- ☐ Have high-tech and low-tech work ready for students.
- ☐ Adjust expectations.

Pembroke Publishers ©2021 *What's the Difference?* by Amanda Yuill ISBN 978-1-55138-348-4

4

Helping Autistic Students with Emotional Regulation

But I Wasn't Finished!

When Schiller told him it was time to pack up, the high-school student picked up the computer and threw it across the classroom, hitting another student. Even though Schiller would give him 15-minute, 10-minute, and 5-minute warnings that it would soon be time to go, this transition continued to be a major trigger for the student for the next year and a half. One day, Schiller realized that, as a teenager, this student liked to be in control (because who doesn't?) and so instead of telling him it would soon be time to go, she asked him if he thought it was almost time to stop writing on the computer. It took a while, but he was able to agree that he guessed it was time to go. Schiller learned that for this student, questions were much better received than statements and helped reduce triggers.

For more on Zones of Regulation, see zonesofregulation.com

Dr. Stuart Shanker, a leading authority on self-regulation, says that self-regulation is the ability to manage and recover from stress (Shanker, 2012). Using this framework, emotional regulation is the ability to manage our emotions and recover from emotional stress. A trigger is something that causes a student emotional stress that can lead to a sensory correction, which sometimes leads to the student or others being hurt, as in Schiller's classroom. Therefore, it is important to teach students how to regulate their emotions and recognize triggers before a computer is thrown across the room again. Perhaps the most well-known approach for teaching children emotional regulation is called Zones of Regulation, which divides emotions into four zones. It teaches students to recognize which zone they are in (e.g., blue for sad or tired; green for happy; yellow for agitated; red for angry) and how to return to a more contented state.

Triggers

Autistic students can experience stress for a variety of reasons, including when their sensory system is overloaded or when something unexpected happens. Here are some common triggers:

- Sights: lights that are too bright or flashing, patterns that are too busy, over-crowded classroom walls, things that move quickly
- Sounds: loud sounds, buzzing noises, sudden sounds, raised voices
- Touch: itchy clothing tags, sticky seats, lack of tactile sensory input
- Smells: bad smells, overpowering smells, smells they don't prefer
- Tastes: having something for lunch they don't want to eat
- Transition: going to/leaving school, changing activities or classrooms (especially if they were not finished the previous activity), starting or ending recess
- Unexpected events: fire drills, assemblies, interruptions, lockdowns
- Required, non-preferred tasks: being asked to put away toys/phones, being asked to do schoolwork/homework
- Unmet needs: the need for food, exercise, quiet, sleep, sensory input; not being able to communicate their needs
- Fear: of insects, people, hairbrushes, new situations, angry teachers
- Other students: when students in the classroom purposely trigger a student

And many, many more.

There are many signs that can help us know when a student is being triggered:

- Self-stimulation: rocking, flapping, humming, walking around, repeating words or phrases, tapping, touching the same thing over and over
- Anger: reddened neck and face, loud voice, yelling/screaming, exaggerated hand movements, stamping feet, clenching fists or jaw
- Restlessness: inability to stay seated or stand in one place, repeated actions (e.g., opening and closing their school bag or a book)
- Loss of abilities: loss of speech, ability to think clearly, self-control, communication, clear eyes (they become glazed), reasoning

<aside>A reminder that, in an effort to use more positive terminology in this book, *sensory correction* is used instead of *meltdown* (as recommended by Lovering Spencer).</aside>

As teachers, if we can identify the triggers that lead to a sensory correction, we can work on reducing or eliminating them. Lovering Spencer reads the student's IEP and asks parents about a student's triggers in order to reduce them. Ronca says that he is like a stress detective, finding out what causes his students stress. Schiller uses her intuition and patience to figure out what her students' triggers are. This takes time and effort. Obviously, some triggers cannot be eliminated, like the need for the student to go home at the end of the day. Sometimes parents can also have triggers; for example, if I am a bit late dismissing the students, I tell parents, "Don't worry, I will not keep anyone overnight. I am sending them all home." Sometimes humor can deflect triggers!

Our students are not the only one with triggers. As teachers, we also have triggers, things that cause us stress. It is good to know your own triggers so you can avoid them or at least be aware when you are being triggered. If you are going to ask your students to self-regulate, you need to demonstrate that for them. You cannot have a temper tantrum because the Starbucks barista gave you decaffeinated coffee that morning, even though they serve you the same order—regular coffee—every morning … *every morning*.

<aside>See page 66 for a checklist for Helping Autistic Students with Emotional Regulation.</aside>

I Just Can't Handle My Life!

She didn't want to leave the live fish in the aquarium at the grocery store and so the student flopped down on the floor and screamed. At this point, an elderly woman informed the teacher that his child was a brat (cue knowing nods of parents of autistic children everywhere). The teacher, in turn, informed the woman that his student was autistic and the woman backed down. As Beth Cubitt, mother of two autistic children, knows, it is not always possible to avoid loud, messy sensory corrections, even if we have recognized the triggers. People who don't know any better will judge, and people who do know better will sympathize and they will be glad it's not them dealing with the situation today!

When autistic students have a sensory correction, they are often unable to control themselves. Their self-regulation is unavailable to them and they become so overwhelmed that it's like their brain shuts off or their nervous system is overloaded. Often they don't even remember what they have done—for example, trashing the office—and may wonder why their father is there. Other times, they feel horrible about what they have done, especially if it involves hurting others or destruction of property, and might be excessively worried about being in trouble. Later, they may be embarrassed that they, say, ran down the hall thinking they were on fire during a fire drill. Part of self-regulation is helping students process what happened so they are able to let it go, move on, return to the class, and learn again.

As mentioned before, the first step is to keep sensory corrections from happening. Learning triggers, helping students recognize their own triggers, teaching emotional regulation, and knowing what is in the IEP and the safety plan (if there is one) are all ways to prevent a student from becoming triggered and then overwhelmed. When you first notice the trigger is the best time to remind a student of the strategies you have talked about and practiced to help them calm down. This can include listening to music, going to a sensory corner or room, breathing deeply, going for a walk, or using a fidget toy. It's important to remember to remain calm if a student is escalating their behavior—raising your voice or reacting will not help them or you. Ronca advises to respond, "That's okay," when they say they hate you. (Parents may have some experience with this.) Kyriakides relates that it is helpful to remember that students with Asperger's can seemingly escalate from being fine to being overwhelmed quite quickly, whereas students who are less verbal might show more indicators that they are escalating; e.g., flapping.

A strategy seen at autistic conferences to avoid becoming overwhelmed is the use of a color-coded name-tag system (Silberman, p. 448). Each participant choses a name tag of a different color to indicate their desired level of interaction. A red name tag means they do not want any interaction. A yellow name tag means they want to interact only with those they know. A green name tag means they are okay for spontaneous social interaction. Participants are able to display a name tag of whichever color signifies how they are feeling at that point. They can change their name tag at any time if how they are feeling changes. This could be modified to work in a classroom so that students could first learn to distinguish how they are doing each day, and then use a name tag or a card to indicate what level of interaction they feel comfortable with that day: red for no interaction; yellow for the teacher only, or perhaps the teacher and one friend; and green for anyone. Okay, now I know you are thinking of someone who should wear a red name tag every day, but let's be kind…

When, despite our best efforts and the best efforts of the student, a student has a sensory correction, the first thing to do is to make sure that all students are safe. You might need to move students or objects out of the way (maybe it wasn't the best day to work on sculpting clay…). If there is a safety plan, this is the time to enact it. The plan might include allowing the student to go to a quiet room, for a walk, or to see an educational assistant or a certain teacher. Welker suggests that, if a student is having difficulty calming down, two people can have a conversation near them (so that they can hear it) about something that interests the student. The conversation might entice the student into that conversation and help them calm down, or at the very least distract them. It is important to remember to try any strategy for a while before giving up on it; it could take a couple of months for it to work for an autistic student, whereas with other students it might take only a couple of weeks.

When the student is calm again, it is important to talk with them about the sensory correction—why it happened and what to do if the same thing happens again. It's good to let them know that we know they are doing their best and that they were obviously overwhelmed. Allow the student to apologize and reassure them that your relationship is not broken or damaged. Next, remind them of your talks about emotional regulation, about recognizing the thing that triggered them and how to catch it before they are overwhelmed the next time. Together with the student, take some time to practice de-escalation strategies or calming techniques; e.g., positive self-talk or doing a puzzle. I often try to end the talk with a joke or a laugh. Sometimes I try to sing the song they use to calm down, but I sing it very badly on purpose. This way, the student will feel that it is safe to talk to me again the next time they have a sensory correction—although perhaps not safe to do karaoke.

That's Not Rebellion, It's Anxiety

Robison tells of visiting a relative in a psychiatric ward:

> When my mother took me to see him, a nurse with a key let us into his room. I had not realized they could lock people up in a hospital. I resolved to be even more careful whenever my mom took me to the doctor. (Robison, 2007, p. 14)

Anxiety is invisible. Anxious behavior is visible. *Very* visible! It is easy to attribute anxious behavior to rebellion. It looks like the student is doing what they want to do, instead of what we have asked them to do. I mean, how many times can you say, "Don't chew your pencils"? It is essential to remember that anxiety can be playing a big role in challenging behavior. If we can find the source of the anxiety and prevent it—or at least curtail it—we can prevent or reduce the anxious and problematic behavior. Even if we cannot eliminate the source of the anxiety, just acknowledging the anxiety and/or the source of the anxiety can help reduce challenging behavior. The goal is for our students to experience less anxiety and for us to experience fewer soggy pencils.

Most of the time, we are not aware that our students are feeling anxiety, but they are. One teacher felt that 95% of his day was spent helping his autistic students manage their anxiety. At the Chiefs of Ontario Conference (2019), Dr. Sonia Mastrangelo said that anxiety and stress in children with ASD is included in the diagnosis as the most debilitating problem, as their response is fight, flight, freeze, or faint. It looks like rebellion, but it's really anxiety.

It can be difficult to distinguish between defiance at doing the work and a refusal to do work due to anxiety. Here are a few examples:

- A Grade 8 student was asked to do a song book of her life, which was to be shared with the class. She refused to do the work because she didn't want to share private things about her life with the class. She wasn't disengaged, rebellious, or lazy; she was frozen with anxiety, unable to move forward.

- Another student was having a lot of difficulty with writing while working on an assignment. When he made a mistake, he stopped working and refused to go on. He wasn't lazy or even bored; he thought that he would never be able to do the assignment because writing it was too difficult. This anxiety caused him to freeze.
- When an autistic student was asked to do work he felt he couldn't do, he would leave the classroom. His response to anxiety was flight.

At times, we might not realize our students are dealing with anxiety; Cook observes that at other times, it will be very clear. Some autistic students will speak out their inner thoughts all the time. Things other people would keep inside, our autistic students might say out loud. Yes, it can be awkward, annoying, irritating, or seemingly rude; however, there is a beauty to it as well. Cook encourages teachers to validate the student's feelings. Say things like, "I understand how you could feel anxious about that," or "I have been frustrated by difficult work too." Try to ignore the part where they called you names, as it was also part of the anxiety—even though we might be a bit self-conscious about our "Dumbo ears."

Besides validating our students' feelings, there are many strategies we can use to help them deal with their stress. Ronca emphasizes that we need to be the calm person in the midst of what is going on around our students at any time. They need a person they can trust at all times in order to feel safe (even though they said that we not only had Dumbo ears, but we also were as big as Dumbo, and they offered us a feather). More than with other students, we need to be calm to help autistic students overcome their anxiety and be able to learn.

Physical touch can also help students reduce their anxiety. Grandin (2013) created a "squeeze machine" that she crawled into, which squeezed her sides; it helped her calm down. Robison (2007, p. 16) says that he also likes having things press on him. If possible, have weighted vests or weighted blankets in the room for students to put on when they are anxious. Otherwise, they can put on their backpacks, with heavy books inside, and walk around. It would just be coincidence if it was the end of the day and the student was also helping you carry those books to your car…

Kluth and Schwarz (2008, p. 89) recommend using the power cards developed by Alisa Gagnon. Each card has a story of a person who has overcome a problem; e.g., learning to shake hands instead of always hugging people (there is an age limit for the appropriateness of hugging everyone). On the other side of the card are a few points to remind the student how to do that task. When students are feeling anxious about doing that thing, they can use the power card to help them. Multiple copies of the same power card can be placed in strategic places around the classroom.

Remember we discussed students' favorite things? Well, these items can be used to help calm down students. I remember one student loved uncooked rice and carried a margarine container of it with him everywhere he went. When he felt anxious, he would run his hands through the rice and it would make him feel better. Students can carry a stuffed animal or a favorite keychain, or they can listen to favorite music. Chocolate always makes me feel less anxious… On the TV show *Atypical*, the main character, who is autistic, recites the four types of penguins when he is anxious. In fact, if a student has something they say to help them feel calm, other students in the class can say it with them or can encourage the autistic student to start saying it when they notice that student feels anxious. Mine might be, "Dark, Milk, White, Semisweet."

One of my friends has a son who was diagnosed with autism and generalized anxiety disorder. She explains that if we thought the world was attacking us, we would be anxious too! Autistic people often reveal that they feel this world was not made for them (check out wrongplanet.net). Kohlemeier wants to tell all teachers, "I promise you, he did not get up this morning with the purpose of pissing you off. Don't take it personally. He looks like other kids but he's not following the rules. Teachers forget. He is autistic. He is anxious." It is anxiety, not rebellion, and it is often easy for us to forget that. That is why it is important to remember.

Breathe In 1-2-3, Breathe Out 1-2-3

I was teaching Kindergarten and I was dropping off some papers for another Kindergarten teacher while her class was at centres. Her class was so quiet! They played so nicely! Even the boys at the blocks centre! When I asked her how she did that, she told me that when she was introducing centres at the beginning of the year, she showed them how to play quietly and told them, "This is how you play in a Kindergarten classroom." For the first two weeks of the school year (at least), she went around and reminded children to play quietly during centres. I went back to my Kindergarten classroom and I started with her plan right away, even though it wasn't the beginning of the year. I explained how to play quietly in centres. I reinforced the lesson for the next couple of weeks and then periodically when children would get loud again. It was revolutionary for me (and probably for some of the children who were sensitive to noise). From then on, I had much quieter classrooms, even when I taught Grade 7! A calm class atmosphere can really help autistic students with self-regulation and staying calm, or with regaining calm when they've lost it.

The atmosphere in the classroom starts with the teacher. I am really more of a fun, loud, enthusiastic teacher than a calm, quiet, soothing teacher. So when my students need some calm, I have to concentrate on becoming a calmer teacher. This takes some effort on my part. I have to lower my voice, move slowly, take more pauses when I speak, and demonstrate how to be calmer. Even more difficult than that, I have to maintain the calm temperament for a period of time and not revert to my loud voice and joking character at the first giggle, which is my natural instinct. Of course, there is a time for loud, enthusiastic jokes in a classroom (thank goodness) and there is a time for quiet, peace, and serenity. As the excellent teachers that we are, it is our job to know the difference.

Naturally, this is easy to do when things are going well. The challenge is to remain calm when students aren't responding, when we are getting frustrated and yell at students, "Just put on your coat. It shouldn't take 15 minutes in Grade 6!" (Okay, so maybe that's just me…) Yelling will not work and only makes things worse. Maintaining a calm atmosphere means that we maintain our calm, even when the circumstances are anything but. This includes treating our students well, even when they are not treating us well. Of course, it is okay to state our boundaries—"Please don't spit at me"—and we want to be calm while we state them. We want to make sure everyone is taking a break when they need it, including ourselves. This might mean allowing an autistic student to play games on the tablet for 10 minutes, even when it is not indoor recess. More than simply remaining calm, we want to try to figure out what is going on with our students so we can help them return to a calm, spitless state themselves.

- Schiller reminds us that we need to be friendly and courteous, and to help our students to feel special, even when things aren't going well—even when the students do not respond, "Good morning, Ms. Yuill," for months.
- Rathee says we need to remain calm even when the students are swearing at us. It is not personal, she says, and she's right. It feels personal—very personal—but it isn't. She recommends just watching and staying back a bit, and then, as

they calm down, slowly going to them and distracting them; for example, you might ask a question about something unrelated. She says that even if they say they don't like us at first, they will get used to us; it just takes time.

- Ronca reminds us to make sure we take a break when we need it so we don't get worked up and frustrated.
- Hucklebridge says that we need to remember to respect the emotions our students have that we can't see. Autistic students have huge emotions and they may not choose to share them with us. The student might not look us in the eye and they might not answer us, and, in this case, we need to think, "What do they need?" They may not be able to tell us that they need something, but their actions are making it very clear.

If any of your students also have ADHD, it will be almost impossible for them to be calm and quiet if they have not had enough exercise. Adequate exercise is essential for emotional regulation (also it helps regulate sleep, weight, and finances—okay, not finances). Schiller finds that exercise is the only way some autistic children can get rid of pent-up emotions—huge, pent-up emotions. Sometimes, the time they have to exercise over recess or lunch will not be enough and they will still need more exercise. When I have this kind of student, I implement 10 minutes of exercise as soon as students get to school, after each recess, and after lunch. This might seem like a lot of time; however, it really saves time in the end because I am not dealing with as many behavioral issues in the classroom.

OPHEA.net has lots of great ideas for physical activities.

One year I had my Kindergarten class run around the playground in laps until the children started to sit down. They loved it! Another year, my intermediate class worked on a dance routine, of which we learned a bit more every day. Some of them loved it. These children need constant running or moving. Playing tag or other games does not provide enough activity, because the students are not constantly running, and some students are trying to stand where we can't see that they are just standing around—like on the soccer field, where there is nowhere to hide… These students need to be moving constantly, at a good pace, for 10 minutes. With junior classes, I sometimes take everyone outside and I have them run and touch a tree, then touch a wall, then something blue, then someone else's shadow, etc. Then, after the exercise, we go back to the classroom and do 5 to 10 minutes of mindfulness, reading, or something else that helps them calm down. Shelley Murphy's book *Fostering Mindfulness: Building skills that students need to manage their attention, emotions, and behavior in classrooms and beyond* gives many ideas for this part of the day.

Practicing these two things—exercise and a calming activity—any time students come into the classroom from a break can make a huge difference in the atmosphere of a classroom. Many educators, including Rathee, say that students especially need help with emotional regulation and staying calm after lunch. Why, why do students always want to wrestle right after lunch? If it is only the autistic student who needs the exercise and you need more instructional time with the class, Rathee recommends arranging with the physical education teacher for the autistic student to come to the gym for ten minutes after lunch to exercise.

Although I have already mentioned this before, it bears repeating: an essential part of a calm atmosphere in a classroom with autistic students is a sensory corner in the classroom, if there is not a Snoezelen room (or similar room) in the school. A sensory corner can be a quiet reading corner, a pup tent, or any place where the students can feel like they are alone. Who knows? If the principal knows about the space, she may come and use it too! Cubitt's daughter needs to have time to herself, away from a situation that's bothering her. Like many other autistic children, she knows when she needs space and will make use of the sensory corner if it is available. Lansimaki recommends this space have a beanbag chair, lava-lamp lights, dollar-store balls that light up, and headphones and music. In her "safe place," Ngui has a rug with tactile dots, a picture of how to breathe, a mirror, and pictures of faces that are angry, frustrated, sad, etc. so that students can figure out how they are feeling. Other items in the sensory corner could include books, a puzzle, a coloring book, a stuffed animal, and a pillow. If there is no space, try using a light-colored table cloth that be draped over a student's desk so they can sit underneath their desk, be alone, and still have enough light to read. As you get to know your students, you can customize your sensory corner to their needs. This corner works only if the student is allowed to go there when they need to. It is not an incentive or a reward, but a place to be calm so they can regulate their emotions.

Calming Activities

There are many calming activities that students can do when they are upset. The key is to find the activities that work well for your students. Some students yell into a pillow or rip up paper and then feel calm, whereas other students find that those activities simply fuel their anger. You might discover that your student calms down when they blow bubbles, breathe with an expandable ball, or breathe in a scent, whereas other students might not be able to sit still to do these activities. Alternatively, you could find that some students need to squeeze something, or hold a stuffed animal or a hot water bottle, and others need to talk or to be left alone. There are many, many ways to calm down, just as there are many, many students. Finding a good fit for each student is an important way to maintain a calm class atmosphere. Think about yourself and what helps you stay calm, or your family or friends and what helps them stay calm. I like to talk with a friend, pray, and exercise. You should definitely not hug me or touch me when I am upset, as that will not help me calm down—just FYI.

See page 19 for more on pets in the classroom.

If you have tried everything else and are unable to help your student be calm, try a class pet. It will almost definitely be worth it. As I have mentioned, very brave teachers have classroom pets, which can be excellent tools to help students with emotional regulation. Mandic's first friend in class was a bunny. Mandic first read to the bunny and then was more open to friends in the class. Ngui recommends fish as a calming influence. Some children might come to school with their own therapeutic pet; dogs are, of course, the most common. These pets are trained to help their owner and can even tell when their owner is going to have a seizure if they have epilepsy. There are programs that use horseback riding as a therapy; although you will not have horses in your classroom (due to the obvious space and toileting problems), you might be able to arrange for a field trip to a riding stable.

You're Important!

More than simply helping our students survive school, we want to help them thrive. Helping students with emotional regulation is not simply knowing how to deal with difficult emotions, it is also helping to build their emotional maturity.

This includes self-esteem. We want our students to grow, not only in knowledge and skills, but also in confidence and self-esteem. Tom describes a situation when he was in high school and a Child and Youth Worker (CYW) was assigned to work with him. When he was not doing well in school, it was attributed to him and not the CYW. However, when he was doing well in school, it was attributed to the CYW and not to him. Obviously, we want to avoid this kind of situation. Praise students for their own work and build their self-esteem.

There are a few things that are often seen in classrooms that can really affect the self-esteem of our autistic students. The first one we want to avoid is sending our autistic students to the office when they (or we) need help. Even though this might be to give them a chance to calm down, it is seen as a punishment. It would be better to make an arrangement with the librarian, gym teacher, or Kindergarten teacher that allows your student to go to their room for a few minutes when they need a break. This can help you have a better reputation at the office, as well. Another thing often seen in classrooms is the whole class being given points for good behavior and having points taken away for bad behavior. Often autistic students don't like to be singled out, especially for negative reasons. It can really hurt self-esteem if a child is often being singled out as the reason the class is losing points, free time, etc. Even if the points are simply for the individual student and not the whole class, this may not be the best method for autistic students.

Rathee says that, in her experience, autistic students remember everything. When we give them respect, make them proud of themselves, and help to improve their self-esteem, they remember that. When we catch a student doing something positive and comment on it, this can really boost students' self-esteem. (With each child, find out if it would be okay to tell the whole class the positive information or if the student would prefer you share it with them privately.) Coombs recommends having students be helpers by wiping the whiteboard clean, lining up the winter boots, helping classmates carry something heavy, or reading to younger students. Rathee reminds teachers to appreciate the things our students do and to let them know it; you might say, "I'm so glad all of the coats are hung up today and none are on the floor," or "I'm so glad everyone has their phone off their desk and is ready for the test," or "I'm so glad everyone remembered to take home their milk from snack program instead of leaving it out on the desk overnight."

Lesson Plan: Practicing Emotional Regulation

Review Emotional Regulation Strategies

The purpose of this lesson plan is to give students opportunities to practice emotional regulation when they are calm in order to make it easier to practice the same strategies when they are upset.

1. As a class, make a list of calming methods that you have discussed as a class or that students know themselves. For example,

   - Breathing in for 3, breathing out for 3
   - Listening to music
   - Removing themselves from the situation
   - Reading a book
   - Talking with a friend
   - Thinking positive thoughts: "It will be okay. This will get worked out."
   - Going for a walk
   - Drinking water

- Using a fidget toy
- Writing down/Coloring their feelings

2. Discuss how each one works.

Role Play

1. Have students break into partners and use the script on page 65 to role-play a situation where emotional regulation could be very difficult. Ask the student role-playing B to actually do the calming exercise at the end of the role-play.
2. Have students practice the role-play a couple of times each so that each student has a chance to try a couple of calming strategies.
3. When students have had about 10 minutes to practice, ask them to do the role-play as though they were very happy, then sad, then angry. You can also try it in different styles: e.g., opera style, cowboy style, etc. Give students 10 more minutes to try the role-play in a certain style, still doing the calming techniques at the end.
4. Have students perform the dialogue in their favorite style, complete with the calming strategy at the end.
5. Discuss how this could help students in a situation in which they are upset.

Emotional Regulation Role-Play

Practice this dialogue with a partner. At the end, practice a calming strategy: for example, deep breathing; going for a walk; positive self-talk; listening to music; reading a book; talking with a friend; etc.

A: Hi! How's it going today?

B: Good, good. How about you?

A: I'm good. Hey, can I borrow your eraser for my next class? I'll bring it back after that.

B: No, I'm sorry, I need my eraser for my class.

A: Please? I promise I'll bring it back!

B: I believe you, really I do! It's just that I need it for my next class.

A takes the eraser and runs off.

B is unable to follow because the class is starting and the teacher is unavailable. B chooses a calming technique and does it.

Pembroke Publishers ©2021 *What's the Difference?* by Amanda Yuill ISBN 978-1-55138-348-4

Helping Autistic Students with Emotional Regulation: Checklist

Recognizing Triggers

- ☐ Use Zones of Regulation.
- ☐ Ask parents and read the IEP.
- ☐ Be patient and persevere.
- ☐ Be aware of your own triggers.

Preventing Sensory Corrections

- ☐ Use positive language.
- ☐ Don't judge.
- ☐ Learn triggers.
- ☐ Work with students to regulate their emotions.
- ☐ Remain calm and use a soothing voice.
- ☐ Use color-coded tags or some other system for students to indicate the level of engagement they are prepared for.
- ☐ Remember that students with Asperger's might not give indications they are being triggered as other autistic students do; e.g., flapping, etc.

Dealing with Sensory Corrections

- ☐ Make sure all students are safe; remove students/objects from danger.
- ☐ Follow the safety plan/IEP.
- ☐ Call for help if needed; allow student to go to another teacher or for a walk.
- ☐ Distract the student.
- ☐ Have a conversation near them that will interest them to try to engage/distract them.
- ☐ When the student is calm, talk to them about what happened without judging.
- ☐ Reassure the student that your relationship is not damaged.
- ☐ Go over de-escalation techniques and practice them.

Anxiety

- ☐ Validate the student's feelings: "I understand how you could feel that way."
- ☐ Use weighted vests or weighted blankets, which might help decrease the student's stress.
- ☐ Use favorite things, which might help decrease the student's stress.
- ☐ Use power cards to help students overcome anxiety about specific tasks.
- ☐ Remember that students are not trying to frustrate you. It's not personal.

Maintaining a Calm Atmosphere

- ☐ Speak at a lower volume, slowly; move more slowly; and concentrate on being calm for a period of time.
- ☐ Be friendly and courteous, even when things aren't going well.
- ☐ Leave the student alone to calm down; watch them to keep them safe.
- ☐ When the student is calmer, approach them and try to distract them; have patience, as it can take time.
- ☐ When students are not responding, consider what they might need to help them be calm.
- ☐ Make sure students have a lot of exercise, followed by mindfulness, silent reading, or other calming techniques.
- ☐ Have a sensory corner or a Snoezelen room.
- ☐ Have a class pet.

Building Self-Esteem

- ☐ Do not always send autistic students to the office; arrange for them to go to the library, Kindergarten room, etc. when they need a break.
- ☐ Do not take points or privileges away from the class because of something the autistic student does.
- ☐ Catch your students doing something positive and give rewards or let the class know.
- ☐ Have the student be a helper.
- ☐ Show appreciation for the everyday things the student does.

Pembroke Publishers ©2021 *What's the Difference?* by Amanda Yuill ISBN 978-1-55138-348-4

5

Helping Autistic Students with Communication

Communication Detectives

As a teenager and young adult, I taught swimming lessons to fund my university degrees. One of the places I taught is called Variety Village, a charity with a sports complex that is a "community that transforms lives through inclusive physical activity and education." One of the little boys in one of my swimming classes was nonverbal and loved the water. He always wanted to put his face in the water; however, he did not have the physical ability to raise his face out of the water. I had to keep an eye on him in order to raise his face out of the water when he put it in—which was a lot! I started noticing that, when I raised his face out of the water, he was inattentive and wouldn't smile, something he did the whole rest of the class. I talked with his teacher and asked if it was possible that the light reflecting on the water was causing petit-mal seizures. It turned out he did have seizures and he wasn't putting his face in the water on purpose; he was having a seizure and going limp. He was unable to tell us and I had to use my detective skills to figure it out. Even though this was happening, he still loved the water and had great fun every class. We arranged to have an assistant swim instructor in the water with him for the whole class after that.

The definition of autism, according to Autism Speaks, includes challenges with social skills and nonverbal communication. Many autistic people have challenges with communication, not only those who are minimally verbal. The strategies presented here for use with minimally verbal students can also help those who can communicate with words and sentences. Also, it is becoming increasingly likely that minimally verbal autistic students will be integrated into mainstream classrooms to a greater degree. As you might not have an educational assistant or any other help, especially for the full day, it is important to consider how to teach these students in an equitable and enjoyable way. Lea tells of teaching a minimally verbal student, a new experience for her. He spoke only in words and phrases, not in sentences, and mostly used nonverbal communication. Fortunately, she was able to rely on the help of a Special Needs Assistant (SNA) in her

See page 77 for a checklist for Helping Autistic Students with Communication.

first experience teaching a minimally verbal student. I, too, had someone help me in one of my first experiences with a minimally verbal student who was blind and had a full-time caregiver, who explained that the student made maps of her surroundings in her mind. She loved it when you would walk with her, put her things down, and then walk with her somewhere else. She would hold your hand and take you back to her things, using the map in her mind. It was a fun game for her and for me.

Problems with Communication

There is no one problem with communication that all autistic people have; there are many different problems, and some autistic people have no difficulty with communication at all. It helps to understand some of the more common issues so that we may be better able to help our students. Grandin (2013, p. 89) lists four common auditory processing problems:

1. language input: the autistic student cannot hear hard consonants so they are unable to make sense of the words, or they hear the words but are unable to connect them to the meaning
2. language output: the autistic student is unable to get the words out
3. attention-shifting slowness: the student is unable to shift attention from the person speaking, to other noise, and then back to the person speaking quickly enough to understand the sentence
4. hypersensitivity to sound: sounds like loud voices might physically hurt their ears

As teacher-detectives, we may notice that our minimally verbal student moves away from students who are yelling and this might lead us to talk to them in a very quiet voice. Alternatively, we may notice that they are easily distracted by other noises in the classroom, and so we might ask the class to be especially quiet when we are speaking with our autistic student. If language output is the problem, we could have certain common phrases programmed on a tablet that the student can press and the tablet will speak out for them (in an Australian accent, if you wish).

My sister's mother-in-law has poor vision. She was out with her granddaughters (my nieces) one day at the store, looking at stuffies. Her granddaughter had been right behind her, but moved to look at something else, and another lady stood where the granddaughter had been. The grandmother's working memory (or short-term memory) told her that her granddaughter was there, so she took a stuffed frog, turned around, and said, "ribbit, ribbit" to a stranger. Her working memory served her well; it was her eyesight that failed her. Working memory supports language comprehension and communication. Habib et al. (2019, p. 1) found that, "individuals with ASD demonstrate large impairments in working memory." One year, when I was teaching instrumental music to intermediate students, I taught an autistic boy how to read music. As he was visual, we were using a keyboard for him to learn the names of the notes. I taught him where middle C is on the keyboard and then D. However, when I introduced E, he could no longer name D. He could only hold two items in his working memory at once. We had to practice C and D until they were in his long-term memory, and then I could introduce E.

It is very difficult to communicate if you cannot remember the name of the thing you want to talk about. Memory is something that gets better with practice so, when we are helping our students to communicate, we need patience. They might just need more repetitions of something in order to remember it. As working memory plays a role in social cognition, even if a minimally verbal student has no problem with language in a given situation, the communication can still be an issue due to a misunderstanding of the social situation. As teachers, we might need to explain social norms to our autistic students and be willing to explain the same thing many times, in many different ways, in order to help them remember, understand, and communicate well. This can require patience—like when we explain again that, even though the student likes the windows open, we are not going to open them when it is snowing outside.

It is important to distinguish between understanding and expressing. Mastrangelo (2009, p. 36) found that expressive and receptive communication may not be at the same level in autistic children. So students might able to explain themselves well, but that does not mean that they understand when we explain something to them. They might be hearing all the details, but are unable to understand the whole (Mastrangelo, 2009, p. 37). Alternatively, simply because they cannot speak does not mean that they don't understand us. Meloche warns teachers not to talk about private matters in front of minimally verbal students. Often, they can understand and might, say, communicate to their parents via a tablet or other method of communication that your husband has a urinary tract infection.

It could be that, when we are able to help our students communicate, some of the behavioral issues we deal with in the classroom will decrease. Mastrangelo explains that problems with communication can lead to other difficulties, including

> aggressive or self-injurious behavior, restricted, repetitive and stereotyped patterns of behavior, pre-occupation with restricted range of interest, obsessive routines and rituals, repetitive motor mannerism, distress over changes in environment, odd responses to sensory stimuli, difficulties sleeping, toileting, eating. (2009, p. 34)

One of the best things we can do for our students is to have an open mind about how they communicate. I mean, who was the first person who thought pressing lips together communicated love?

Who Needs Words?

When I was teaching swimming lessons at Variety Village, a girl in one of my classes asked me if my name Amanda starts with an *A*. I said yes and asked her what letter is at the beginning of the word *swim*. The teacher overheard us talking and told me not to waste my time. She said she had worked with her autistic students on recognizing first letters of words for a long time and that they couldn't learn. I think she was having a bad day... However, that her student knew my name started with an *A* was proof that they were learning and that the teacher was, in fact, actually teaching them! The truth is that all our autistic students are able to communicate, whether they speak in words, in gestures, or some other way. All teachers have bad days, when we think what we are doing is not making a difference, but our communication with minimally verbal students is making a difference—often more of a difference than we know.

Many minimally verbal autistic children can understand what we're saying; they are simply slower in responding to it than average. Cantiani et al. (2016, p. 23) found that minimally verbal autistic children had relatively intact basic sensory-perception processing skills; however, there was a delay in response time when compared with typically developing children. Instead of responding in their own words, autistic children might respond in gestures or in echolalia. Hucklebridge reports that some children talk using their hands or shoulders, some act out, some scream, and some say nothing. The signs children give can be subtle. A good teacher reviews the subtleties of the student's behavior to find out what they need in order to communicate, and what they are saying when they do communicate, with or without words. And you are a good teacher!

Boff says that she has met teachers who think that minimally verbal autistic students can't learn, and she disagrees. She believes that all autistic students can learn. She tells the story of one minimally verbal student who liked playing with a car. She decided to teach him the phrase, "I want car" so he would be able to state his request. After a while of Boff saying, "I want car," her student would say, "Car." A while later, he could say, "Want car," and finally, "I want car." After that, when he wanted the car, he would say so—often. Clearly, simple repetition was combined with patience and perseverance on the part of both teacher and student to result in learning.

One of the easiest and most fun ways we can help students to communicate is through play. Mastrangelo (2009, p. 36) found that both expressive and receptive language was developed through play. Playing out real-life situations is recommended; e.g., dress-up or role-play. In these situations, the language used in play is the same language used in everyday life (Mastrangelo, 2009, p. 38). For example, you could teach a minimally verbal student to play a matching game, and then have them play it with another student in the class—hopefully a talkative student. You could also encourage younger students to "play house" or "play dress-up." Grandin (2020, Leading Edge Seminar) recommends using concrete examples from everyday life to help students communicate; e.g., using roadkill to encourage students to look both ways for cars before crossing the street. This would definitely be a conversation-starter in my classroom!

Grandin (2013, p. 91) comments that parents and teachers have told her over and over that they have taught children communication through singing. When Kindergarten children have a difficult time remembering how to spell their name, I use a song they know—like "Twinkle, Twinkle Little Star" or "Row, Row, Row Your Boat"—and put the letters of their name into the tune. In one of my Kindergarten classes, all the students knew how to spell one little girl's name because we sang her name song all the time. She would tell the others not to sing, because it was *her* name song. She's quite a bit older now and still remembers her name song. Anything can be set to music: times tables, grammar rules, World War II history.

Some children learn best when they are moving. Rupert Isaacson, author of *The Horse Boy*, tells how his autistic son seemed to come alive and communicated more when riding horses. Mastrangelo (2019, Chiefs of Ontario Conference) tells of a child who would talk only when swinging. If you have a teacher chair with wheels or a rocking chair, consider allowing the student to sit there while working with them on communication skills.

The order that you teach different parts of speech might also make a difference. Mastrangelo (2019, Chiefs of Ontario Conference) recommends teaching students verbs first (e.g., *sit, run, pick up*, etc.) and then moving on to combine the action words with names (e.g., *Trey sits*, *Szendaiyah eats*, etc.). When teaching students verbs, names, or any form of communication, Cubitt says that it's okay to ask minimally verbal students to repeat themselves. Her daughter's feelings aren't hurt if you don't understand her; just say, "I don't understand, can you say that again?"

In high school, students often have at least four educators in one semester, so it is not necessary for each of you to reinvent the wheel of communication. (Remember to limit use of idioms with most minimally verbal autistic students.) Cook reminds teachers to communicate not only with their autistic students, but also with other educators and parents. You can help autistic students communicate by sharing information among educators and parents about what works and what does not work with each student. Although this takes time, it could save each educator time in their own class, as they would not have to figure out how to communicate with one student all over again.

Going Low-Tech

Students who are minimally verbal or maximally verbal (I just made that up, but I think it really describes some students well—and some teachers, too...) can use many low-tech aids to help their communication. Lansimaki comments that many low-tech aids are visual, and this is a great way to help students communicate.

Sign Language

If we find a student is having trouble expressing themself, teaching them useful words in sign language may make our life and their life a lot easier. It's necessary to teach just one word at a time, and it might take a while for the student to learn each word. But learning even ten words can make a world of difference. Common words students sign are *yes, no, go, stop, eat, toilet, please, thank you, drink, more, help, all done, play, ready, quiet, slow,* and *don't*. It is also helpful to teach students how to sign their favorite activities, like video games or soccer.

Using Pictures

A storyboard or a communication board is a small board (often the size of a large book or small desk) with a few pictures on it. The autistic student or the teacher points at the pictures in order to communicate; often the teacher will say the word and point to the picture. Students might have a communication board they use both at home and at school, or they might come with Picture Exchange Communication System (PECS), a popular version of a communication board. The words on the board are similar to the words used in sign language.

Sometimes a teacher will carry pictures on cards on a lanyard around their neck and shuffle through them to find the one they want or the student wants. It is advisable that the communication board and/or lanyard with pictures follow the student to music, gym, and any other class where there is a different teacher, so that all teachers are using the same method of communication. Pictures around the room can be useful; for example, a stop sign at the door, a sign showing how to wash hands at the sink, a sign showing how to put on winter clothes at the cubbies, etc. If you find you don't have the picture you need, you can simply draw it or ask the student to draw what they want to say. Of course, this works only if you are pretty good at guessing drawings ("It's a banana and two oranges... what did you think it was?").

For students with difficulties in processing language, pictures or lists of items they need are also helpful, because if we list the items out loud without writing them down, the student might not be able to process it all and could forget one item. For example, in their cubby there might be a list of items they need to have in their bag before they go home; for example, lunch box, agenda, library book, and pet rock. On their desk could be a list of things they need to take with them to French class; for example, French book, a pencil, an eraser, and a good attitude.

Boff tells of an EA who worked in her classroom who had a page of faces that showed different emotions. She worked with the autistic students all year, to help them use the pictures to express how they were feeling. By the end of the year, some of the children were able to correct her and show her a different picture if she guessed wrong about their feelings. Also, some of the children were able to take her to another child who had taken their toy and show the picture of the sad or angry face. They were learning communication and emotional regulation at the same time.

First/Then Board

Another very common low-tech visual aid used for communication with autistic students is a First/Then board. This is a piece of paper divided in half, with the word *First* at the top of the left half of the paper and *Then* at the top of the right half; it is accompanied by pictures of activities, similar to the ones on the communication board or on the lanyard. The idea is that the student first has to do the activity we choose, and then they can do an activity they choose (or another one we know they will like). For example, there might be a picture of a student writing on the First half of the page, and a student having a snack on the Then half. Tell the student that, *first* they have to do writing and point to the picture of the student writing; tell them that *then* they can have a snack, and point to the picture of the student having a snack. This is often used when students are asking to play, but need to get some work done first. This works especially well in some schools on Friday, as the snack that day is chocolate milk—a student favorite!

Just Point

In the book *Josiah's Fire*, Tahni Cullen describes a method she used to assess what her minimally verbal autistic son was understanding. She would teach him something in a minute or two and then ask a comprehension question about it. Then she would write different answers on each of two pieces of paper and ask him which was the correct answer. He would touch the paper with the answer he thought was correct. For example, she might teach him that butterflies are caterpillars first and they turn into butterflies. Then she would write the word caterpillar on one sheet and tadpole on another. She would ask him which animal turns into a butterfly, a caterpillar or a tadpole. She was amazed to find out that her son was understanding much more than she had thought, and he was happy not to be asked "baby" questions!

Going High-Tech

Time for an "I'm so old…" joke: I'm so old, I was born in the last millennium. I'm so old, I remember the first computer at our elementary school in the library. We had a lesson on how to insert a floppy disk so the computer would do something, like run a program. We all took turns on the one computer learning how to draw a circle (which took about ten minutes) and you had to instruct it to *run* when you wanted it to execute your program. It did not seem so impressive to me. Next, we learned how to tell the computer to repeat commands we gave it, so we could draw a circle in one minute, or fill an entire page repeating the words, *Wonder Woman is better than Batman*. Still not so impressive. Today, however, computers are impressive *and* helpful—not to mention the Internet! In fact, Harvey Blume (1997) commented in the *New York Times*, "The impact of the Internet on autistics may one day be compared in magnitude to the spread of sign language among the deaf."

There are many reasons why high-tech aids can help our autistic students. Tanaka et al. (2017, p. 1) found that it was easier for people with social communication difficulties to use a computer to learn than to directly interact with another person. There were four main reasons computers were preferred:

> 1) such people favor computerized environments because they are predictable, consistent, and free from social demands; 2) they can work at their own speed and level of understanding; 3) training can be repeated over and over until the goal is achieved; and 4) interest and motivation can be maintained through computerized rewards. (Tanaka et al., 2017, p. 2)

Grandin (2013, p. 179) says that she recommends autistic children use tablets or iPads more than computers or laptops, because the keyboard is right on the screen and their eyes don't have to travel as far from the keyboard to the word they are writing. All children now use tablets in school and autistic students don't feel that they stand out when they are using them. Moreover, there are limitless free apps that can be downloaded to help with almost anything we can think of: math, reading, writing, science, social skills, how to use deodorant (especially relevant for intermediate students after gym class), etc.

For each category, you can find many examples of various programs online. These are ones that many people have recommended.

Recommended Online Programs

Dictation Programs

With a dictation tool like Google Voice Typing (on Google Docs, under Tools), the student talks and the tool writes it on the document. You have to tell it where to put periods and other punctuation; however, it does capitalize the first word of the sentence and proper nouns. Other dictation programs include Dragon Professional Individual and Apple Dictation.

Text-to-Speech Programs

Google Read and Write will read what is written on the screen to the student, and write down what the student dictates. Bookflix is a site that is basically like Netflix for books. Many of the books have text-to-speech programs that read the book to the student. Of course, you can also find many books read aloud on YouTube.

Of course, there are also some difficulties with technology, the first being that there are wait-lists to get access to devices like laptops for children who need them. There is a lack of professionals to train the students. And sometimes, even when we go through all of this, the student does not want to use the technology that we spent countless hours filling out paperwork to get! Kluth and Schwarz (2008, p. 21) tell of having to put information about monster movies into a communication device to get a student interested in it. On the other hand, some students will not put down their device, and this can also be a problem. Many teachers and parents have hidden a tablet at the end of the day so that the next morning, the student would do something else!

That's Funny Because…

"The behavior, condition, and appearance of the source material of any girl under consideration will tell you a lot about what you will have twenty-five years hence," writes Robison (2007, p. 251). He doesn't realize that this is funny, not only what he is saying (if you want to know what your wife will be like in the future, look at her mother), but also how he is saying it. Robison's wife is one of three sisters, and he doesn't understand why he's not allowed to wonder if he got the best sister, when he's allowed to wonder if he got the best car or chainsaw (p. 250). This makes us laugh, but Robison is serious. Autistic people are very literal and often their sense of humor is different from that of a neurotypical person.

Sarcastic humor can make students feel like they are the butt of the joke, even if they are not. So it's a good idea to avoid sarcastic humor.

You want to make sure that your students are not feeling left out when everyone laughs, and so you may want to explain jokes if you see your autistic students looking puzzled. It is also very important that students do not think people are laughing at them—as you can see from the Robison example, that can easily happen. Mandic found that teachers who cracked jokes helped him to open up more. Mandic often follows up on jokes, making sure people know it was a joke and how and why it was a joke. He wants to be part of the fun. Lothian helps her autistic students have fun by finding out more about their sense of humor. One of her students insisted he was a king, and so she would call him King, salute and bow to him, and do a dance. He thought it was funny—it tied into his sense of humor and made a connection with him. It's important to get to know your students' sense of humor.

To help your autistic students with humor, point out when you've made a joke, or slip into conversation that what you just said was a joke. I joke around a lot in my classes and I also tend to tease students, depending on the personality of the student. So in September, I'm always asking my classes if I'm joking or if I'm serious. Soon, they get to know that I'm usually teasing or joking. In classes with autistic students, after September, I periodically ask only the autistic students if I'm teasing, to help them remember. For example, when students ask how old I am, I always respond "100 years old," which some believe! With older classes, I tell them the project is 20 pages instead of 2 pages. They look up, surprised, and then I smile and they tell me that I'm not funny! I do love intermediate students. Of course, this is all based on the personality of the class. Some classes or students are not okay with teasing, so I have different kinds of jokes for them.

You might find yourself in many funny situations with your autistic students that they do not think are funny. Be careful to take them seriously and not laugh when they come with concerns or comments that are important to them, or you will lose their trust. For example, Meloche tells how her son went to the principal's office when he was six years old and told her that he didn't want to go to school anymore. She said he had to go to school to get smarter and to get a job. He replied that his parents said he was smart so he was going to finish up Grade 1 and then he would be done. Even though this is very funny, the principal did her best to be serious and to convince him of the advantages of Grade 2. He would not be convinced.

It is good to look out for instances when an autistic student exercises their sense of humor. They might be joking and we do not realize it. This can make us frustrated or mad; however, they are simply showing their humorous personality. Lothian tells of a student who would always skip the numbers 5 and 6 when he was counting. He knew how to count properly, but he did not. Lothian asked if the numbers were missing and he replied that not only were 5 and 6 missing, 18 was missing too! He was purposely joking, but if Lothian hadn't asked about it, she would have missed his sense of humor.

Lesson Plan: Different Ways of Communicating

Charades

The purpose of this lesson plan is to help students consider different ways of communicating when a student is not able to communicate verbally for a variety of reasons; e.g., they do not talk, they are too upset to talk, they do not understand what you are saying, etc.

1. Talk with the class about the possibility of needing to communicate without words. Ask students if they have ever been so upset that they were not able to talk or they were not able to listen well.
2. Ask students if they can think of some gestures they may use in that situation. Play charades with the whole class. Use phrases such as

> I'm hungry.
> I'm thirsty.
> I'm tired.
> Let's go for a walk.
> I don't want to talk.

3. Have students break into groups of four to continue playing charades.

Pictionary

1. Let students know that sometimes pictures can work better than words or gestures when trying to communicate.
2. Play Pictionary with the whole class. Use phrases such as

   Where's the teacher?
   I need help.
   Where is the bathroom?
   I'm angry.
   Do you have a tissue?

3. Have students break up into groups of four to continue playing Pictionary.

Sign Language

1. Discuss the fact that some students might use sign language or know some signs.
2. Give students a Sign Language sheet like the sample below. Students can also visit a website (e.g., https://cudoo.com/blog/most-popular-sign-language-phrases-you-need-to-know/) to learn simple words, such as "please," "toilet," and "yes."
3. Give students time to practice their name and a few words.
4. Have students get into groups of four, show each other their names, and practice some words.

Sign Language Chart: Freepik.com

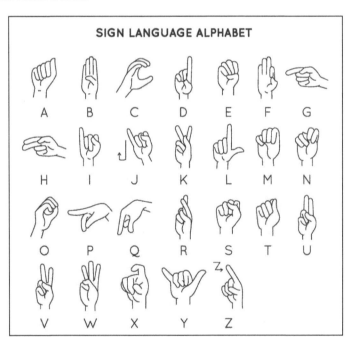

Discuss Nonverbal Communication

1. As a class, discuss various ways of communicating without using words and which ones the students preferred.
2. Ask students if they know of any other ways of communicating without words; suggest storyboards, tablets, pictures on a lanyard, etc.

Strategies to Help with Communication: Checklist

Connecting with Minimally Verbal Students

- ☐ Rely on EAs, SNAs and other educators who work closely with your minimally verbal students for help and advice on communicating with them.
- ☐ Talk in a quiet voice.
- ☐ Make sure the class is quiet when speaking to the student.
- ☐ Program phrases on a tablet that the student can point to when they have difficulty getting the phrase out verbally.
- ☐ Explain social norms to autistic students.
- ☐ Be ready to explain the same thing many times.
- ☐ Be careful what you say in front of minimally verbal students, as they may be able to understand and repeat it later.

Helping Minimally Verbal Students Communicate

- ☐ Adopt an attitude that all children can learn.
- ☐ Use simple repetition, patience, and perseverance.
- ☐ Communicate through play.
- ☐ Act out real-life situations.
- ☐ Use concrete examples from life.
- ☐ Teach through singing.
- ☐ Teach through movement.
- ☐ Teach using animals.
- ☐ Teach verbs first, proper nouns second.
- ☐ If you don't understand what a student is saying, ask them.
- ☐ Have meetings with other educators and parents to share information on the best way to communicate with an autistic student.

Low-Tech Aids

- ☐ Learn some sign language.
- ☐ Use a communication board.
- ☐ Use pictures on a lanyard around your neck.
- ☐ Place pictures around the room.
- ☐ Have the student draw what they want to say.
- ☐ Use pictures of emotions to help students communicate how they feel.
- ☐ Use a First/Then board.
- ☐ After teaching a lesson, write two answers on separate pieces of paper and ask the student to touch the paper with the correct answer.

High-Tech Aids

- ☐ Use tablets, which can be easier for autistic students to use, as their eyes do not have to travel as far from the keyboard to the screen.
- ☐ Use free apps.

Explaining Humor

- ☐ Explain jokes to students.
- ☐ Make sure people are not laughing at autistic students.
- ☐ Explain why people are laughing when a student meant to be serious.
- ☐ Get to know each students' sense of humor to help connect to them.
- ☐ Be clear when you are making a joke.
- ☐ Avoid sarcastic humor.
- ☐ Look for a student's sense of humor.

Pembroke Publishers ©2021 *What's the Difference?* by Amanda Yuill ISBN 978-1-55138-348-4

6

Helping Autistic Students Socialize

Hey, This Is Not the Autism Class!

I remember when an autistic boy was moved from a special education classroom to a mainstream classroom near the beginning of the year. I'll call him Ibrahim. He was goofy, at first, in the mainstream classroom, hiding under desks and behind the coats while the teacher tried to get him ready to go home on the bus. Soon Ibrahim started to imitate the behavior of the other children in the class, mimicking their positive practices. His parents had pushed for the change and the student himself seemed to be okay with the situation. However, the mainstream teacher felt blindsided. She wasn't prepared for a year with a student who was more than three years behind his peers in the curriculum and much further behind in social skills, not to mention the many emails from the parents. She hadn't received any training and was afforded minimal support. It might not be only the autistic student who needs help when transitioning to a mainstream classroom. It might be the teachers, as well, who need help with the transition.

One way to prepare students for the transition from an autism class to a mainstream class is to invite the student to visit the classroom, even if it is a couple of weeks before school starts and there is nobody else there. It helps the student to see where they will be learning. It is also a great idea to take pictures of the classroom and show them to the student, whether they can visit the classroom or not. If possible, give the student a picture of yourself teaching in the classroom. Make it a nice picture—a good-hair-day picture. Before the student transitions to your mainstream class, invite them to visit once a week or even once a day for a couple of months leading up to the transition. Sending a couple of reliable students to the autism class to participate in reading or physical education for a few weeks before the transition can also help the autistic student to feel that they have friends in their new class.

More than merely welcoming our new student into our class, we want to foster a sense of community with them. Craig Goodall, in his article "How to teach Autistic Pupils … by Autistic Pupils," found that inclusion is not necessarily a natural consequence of placing an autistic student in a mainstream classroom. In fact, in his PhD research, autistic students told him that they dreaded mainstream education because of the inflexible teaching, bullying, overwhelming sensory and social overload, and feelings of exclusion and otherness. Moreover, when Goodall (2018, p. 1285) studied autistic people's conceptions of inclusion, he found that, "inclusion is a feeling (a sense of belonging), not a place (mainstream or otherwise)." One way to foster this sense of belonging is to make sure the student has a couple of friends in the class who will help them as they adjust to things. These friends can be their partners during group work. Hancock reminds teachers that autistic students might not like being the centre of attention or pointed out in class. Having friends teach them how the classroom works might be preferable to having teachers do it. Students might give them tips we would not give; e.g., Ms. Yuill hums when she's happy, so that's a good time to ask her for something.

When Hornsby's young son moved into a mainstream classroom, she made a video of herself reading his favorite book and then telling him that he would have a good day. When he was having a difficult time in the class, the teacher would allow him to watch the video and it helped him calm down and made the transition a bit easier.

As with Ibrahim, the behavior of the autistic student might start out being very different from that of most students. It is a good idea to let students know that this might be the case when an autistic student comes, and to give them tools to handle that behavior and still be welcoming. This can be very difficult for students with a strong sense of justice or fairness. "Ms. Yuill, he's sleeping in the sensory corner again—and snoring!" You might have to remind students that each student is given what they need to succeed. We might want to give more incentives to the class as a whole—e.g., free time or extra recess—as everyone is getting used to the transition. While steering the new student in the right direction, remember that it could take a few weeks before they follow the classroom routines and expectations.

Another way to help autistic students transition into a mainstream classroom is to organize some support for them—at least for the first little while. Lansimaki points out that autistic students are used to much lower ratios of teachers to students than in a mainstream classroom, and so having an Educational Assistant or the Special Education teacher come into your classroom for a couple of periods a day can help them ease into the class a bit better. It can also make the transition easier for you as the teacher! This might require some sweet talking on your part to convince your principal that you need the extra help for a while. This is an example of why it's always good to be in the principal's good books.

See page 94 for a checklist for Helping Autistic Students Socialize.

You might try to organize unit plans to cover less-challenging and more-interesting curricula (this is not to say that some curricula are not interesting, she said convincingly) when the autistic student first transitions into your class, in order to give them and yourself time to get used to the new situation without having to deal with a difficult curriculum. It would also be helpful to know the new student's interests and include them in some of the lessons. It is important to remember to give yourself time to adjust and to realize that you might not be able to get as much of the curriculum taught in the first couple of weeks, as you will be helping your new student and your class adjust to the new circumstances. Make sure to have reasonable expectations for your class and yourself, and be prepared to change your expectations as time goes on. Things might move faster or slower than you had originally thought they might. Getting some training, talking with the previous teacher and the parents, and adjusting your expectations can lead to a very positive, profitable outcome for everyone involved, and could help you maintain your good health and positive attitude.

No, a Social Story is Not about Dating (Although it Could Be)

A social story can be a short book, a video, or simply a group of pictures on a piece of paper with a narrative that illustrates situations and problems, and how people handle them. Its purpose is to help autistic people understand social norms and learn appropriate communication. There are social stories about how to make friends, how to play during recess, how to solve conflicts, how to do homework, how to sit in a circle, etc. They are often used with elementary-school children; however, there are social stories for teens as well, though sometimes teens do not want to use them, as they perceive social stories as a tool for young children. Social stories can improve the way in which autistic children socialize and help them learn what to do and what not to do in new situations. Social stories work best when they are read repeatedly. Social stories work best when they are read repeatedly. Social stories work best when they are read repeatedly.

Hornsby's son reads social stories on his own in order to figure things out. She says that social stories are helpful because they break down what is needed for a social interaction, the way an instruction guide would. These are skills that most children pick up on their own, but that some children need to be taught explicitly, like not picking their nose in class. Okay, most children have to be taught that one. When introducing social stories, you might also read Curious George or Amelia Bedelia books. These two characters also need explicit instruction in things that other people understand implicitly. These books can help normalize social stories, and they are fun to read. Who can forget the Man in the Yellow Hat?

Of course, social stories don't work in a vacuum. When a student is having trouble socializing, find a social story about that specific situation and read it with them. Then discuss with them how to apply what they have just read. It is good to read the book at least once a day for the next few days, or until the student is able to apply the concepts in the book. You will probably use a few other strategies as well, with the social story being one part of the solution. In fact, you might find that you use social stories with your whole class; for example, the one on wearing clean clothes and putting dirty clothes in the laundry. Have you smelled those lockers?

Dr. Carol Gray developed social stories and has free samples on her website (https://carolgraysocialstories.com/social-stories/social-story-sampler/). You can also find social stories on YouTube and Teachers Pay Teachers websites. You can make up your own social stories for situations unique to your student; find instructions for making your own social story on the National Autistic Society's website (https://www.autism.org.uk/about/strategies/social-stories-comic-strips.aspx).

Let's Be Friends!

There is a common misconception that autistic students would rather be alone than have friends. Robison (2007, p. 211) says it well:

> I can't speak for other kids, but I'd like to be very clear about my own feelings: *I did not ever* want *to be alone.* And all those child psychologists who said "John prefers to play by himself" were dead wrong. I played by myself because I was a failure at playing with others. I was alone as a result of my own limitations, and being alone was one of the bitterest disappointments of my young life.

Krieger et al. (2018, p. 11) found the same thing in their study—that adolescents want to have friends! And really, do we need studies to tell us that our students want friends? Of course, everyone is unique, and Cubitt explains that her son would be happy by himself in his room all day, although we can take this as the exception and not the rule. Our classroom environment and how we teach our students can support or hinder companionship between our students.

Autism, and especially Asperger's, can be invisible, with no external sign there might be a problem. When autistic students make mistakes with friends or in conversation—for example, telling someone that their breath smells in front of classmates—people tend to think it is a character flaw instead of a manifestation of the autism. It is beneficial to all students if you speak openly about difficulties people can have in conversations and making friends, and how to be charitable and gracious. I like to point out that we want mercy for ourselves and justice for everyone else. I suggest that if we want people to give us a second chance, it is good practice to give others a second chance, too.

In order to help autistic students make friends, the atmosphere in our classroom is of paramount importance. You will be treating your autistic students differently from other students because you will be giving them the support they need in order to succeed, which is different from the support other students need. It is very important that you make it clear that you offer everyone the support they need, that all students have different needs and you are fostering an atmosphere where that is understood and accepted. Schiller states that this is important because, if students think that one student is getting special privileges, they might be jealous of that student and that could prevent them from being friends. This problem is pretty much the same in Kindergarten as it is in Grade 12 (and beyond). As much as possible, we want the help we give our autistic students to be similar to the help we give all our students. Yes, this is a paradox, and it's one each teacher has to answer as best they can in their own classroom.

One thing you can do is to organize opportunities for students to interact. This means that you will choose activities in which students can participate and you choose the groups or pairs of students. This is important because, if students are left to choose for themselves, often the autistic student is left out or chosen last. Even when autistic students are included in an activity, Krieger et al. (2018, p. 18) found that they are on the periphery 71% of the time. In your classroom, you can make sure that these students are part of a group you have chosen for group work. You can organize clubs or teams and invite students to be a part of it. You can make sure students know about clubs or teams within the school, and you can walk them to the event or have another student walk with them at recess, during lunch, or after school. You can let parents know when there are opportunities in the community for their child to participate in sporting events or social clubs, especially if some of the students from your class are already involved. You can try to include the autistic student's special interests in a club you run, or you can see if there are clubs in the community that include their talents or fascinations. It is much easier to interact and make a friend when you have a common interest. Macrame club, anyone?

Students will not always have opportunities to make friends handed to them, and initiating a friendship is another important skill we can teach them. Robison relates the story of trying to make friends:

> At recess, I walked over to Chuckie and patted her on the head. My mother had shown me how to pet my poodle on the head to make friends with him.... The difference between a small person and a medium-sized dog was not really clear to me. (2007, pp. 9, 11)

Younger autistic students might sit or stand by someone with whom they would like to play or be friends, but not know what to do next. There are many social stories about making friends you can read to students. And it is good to choose one that is appropriate for the student and read it to them before every recess. Remind them to walk up to the person with whom they would like to be a friend, look at them, and say that they want to play or to join their group or conversation. It might help to give them the specific words to say and to make an anchor chart they can refer to. Many students can benefit from learning the skill of how to initiate a friendship, and so you might choose to do the anchor chart with the whole class. Another benefit to this is that, when students approach a group to ask to join them, it will be clear to everyone involved what is happening and how to respond. Part of the lesson could be how to allow new people to join in a game that has already started, or how to end a game and start a new game, etc.

Taking Turns

A big part of being able to play well with others is knowing how to take turns. We teach children how to take turns in Kindergarten, even up to Grade 2, but after that we expect students to know how to take turns. The difficulty is that autistic students could still need some help with knowing how to do that. Sometimes the reason students cannot make friends is that they are not yet skilled at waiting their turn. Games like Connect Four are a fun way to teach how to take turns. There are only two players, so neither student has to wait a long time for their turn. It can help to write down *My turn* on a card and *Your turn* on another, and to show them to your autistic student the first few times you play the game. There are also many games you can download on tablets that involve taking turns, if your student is more likely to be engaged by technology. A good time to introduce this concept is during an indoor recess; many students like playing board games during an indoor recess. Be prepared: it could take a while for the student to learn how to take turns, and you might need to focus on that skill in class and outside of class. I remember the first time I played Candyland as a teacher. I probably hadn't played it in more than 20 years. I had forgotten how to play, and the students were excited to be able to explain to me how to play a game. FYI, Candyland is a bit more difficult if you are color blind!

Conversation

Conversation is a skill. If that's new information to you, you're probably naturally skilled at it. Or you may be oblivious to it, as are many autistic students. It is a particularly important skill for high-school students as more and more friendships are based on conversation and fewer and fewer on activities. Robison relays how his Asperger's affected his conversation skills:

> But I had overlooked one key thing: *Successful conversations require a give and take between both people.* Being Aspergian, I missed that. Totally. (2007, p. 11)

Identify one or two mistakes the student is making in conversation and work on those things until the student masters them before moving onto other items. For example, they might not be waiting their turn to talk, or they might be talking too loudly and too closely to the other students. If a student is having trouble with conversation, it is my experience that the other students are not shy about saying what is wrong—she spits in my face when she talks; he never stops talking; he follows me to the bathroom and stands outside the stall talking!

One very common challenge for autistic students in conversation is that they tend to be very blunt and honest, and this is often misinterpreted as rudeness. Hornsby tells of one student who was repeating "chubby cheeks" over and over again. Some girls in his class were angry with him for insulting them, but he was not referring to them. He didn't even know what the phrase meant. He simply liked the sound of it. Other students probably were able to see that the girls were getting upset; however, this student had no idea. Again, if we observe a student having difficulty in one or two areas where people are misinterpreting them as being rude, we can help them work on these things; for example, speaking and then listening instead of speaking and then leaving, or watching people's faces for their response to what we are saying. There are also computer-based social-skills training programs that could be useful for some students. Robison concludes that he still has difficulties with avoiding the appearance of being rude in conversation:

> The only real difference is that I have learned what people expect in common social situations. So I can act more normal and there's less chance I'll offend anyone. (2007, p. 10)

Fostering Friendship

Friendship is a two-way street and so you will most likely be working not only with your autistic students on how to make friends, but also with other students on how to be friends with your autistic students. A tried-and-true method is to pair an autistic student with a caring, accepting, understanding, and trustworthy student. You already know exactly who in your class I'm talking about, don't you? Every class has at least one student who is kind and mature, and who is willing to help most anyone. This student might also draw the autistic student into their circle of friends, providing a group of buddies for the autistic student to get to know. Until the autistic student learns how to initiate social contact, it is best to have the mentor initiate contact, conversation, and play most of the time. Lansimaki suggests encouraging other students to be very open, honest, and blunt with their autistic friend; for example, letting them know how often they would like to hear from them when they are not at school. Do they want to text every night, many times a night, once a week, or only on weekends? I have had this conversation with a few of my friends myself! This can help autistic students feel more secure in the relationship, because they know the expectations clearly. The goal is that both students feel that the friendship is mutually enriching.

Peer Groups Are Great!

Peer groups are a more structured way to help autistic students socialize than pairing them with a kind student in order to foster friendship. Peer groups meet at a certain time every week or every month. They work on specific skills or problems. There are two kinds of peer groups: a peer group for autistic students only and a peer group made up of both autistic and neurotypical students. One teacher ran a peer group for autistic students at her high school once a week over lunch. Her big tip: If you feed them, they will come.

Peer Groups of Autistic Students

At the peer group for autistic students only, mentioned above, they played card games and social thinking games. The main purpose of the group was to enhance social skills, approaches, and etiquette as situations happened in the group. For example, hypothetically, if someone was staring at a female student's chest in an effort to avoid eye contact, the group could discuss how that is socially inappropriate and come up with other places to focus their eyes. The goal was to create a supportive environment where autistic students could use and practice their social skills. It can be very helpful for students to realize that there are others out there who struggle with the same kinds of issues they do. It can make students feel less alone and more encouraged. Running an autistic peer group gives students an opportunity to talk about problems and issues they have in common. It also provides a place where they can be themselves without worrying about how others perceive them. Krieger et al. (2018, p. 23) found that these sorts of peer groups allowed adolescents to form a positive identity and lessened the pressure they felt to fit in.

When planning an autistic peer group, it is best to fit into the student's schedule. Lunch might be an ideal time to host it. As previously mentioned, it is also good to offer food. Incorporating students' ideas into the schedule can help them be more motivated to come each week. For instance, try playing board games for half the time and then video games for half the time. This allows students the opportunity to work on social skills and also ensures that they enjoy themselves and come back. Expect the first few weeks to be a bit disjointed, while everyone figures out what's going on and how the group works. You might want to explain that part of the reason for the group is to help with common issues and problems; be clear about that goal so that students understand it is not simply a social hour, unless you have planned it to be that way. During discussions, you might want to set some ground rules for conversation. Some teachers use a talking stick or conversation ball; only the person holding the talking stick or the conversation ball is allowed to speak. You might need to set a time limit on how long someone can speak. Each group is different and you might find that the group dynamics change over time and perhaps even the purpose of the peer group. At first, it might be just a social group, but it might turn into a support group for dealing with teachers and other students. Or you might find that the social aspect alone is so important you want to forgo the formal discussion. Students like to feel wanted—okay, everyone likes to feel wanted—so be sure to let students know how glad you are that they attend. Not in a fake, TV-weather-person-smile kind of way, but in a sincere, I'm-glad-I'm-not-wasting-my-lunch-doing-this kind of way.

Mixed Peer Groups

The second kind of peer group is a peer group with both autistic and neurotypical students. One very successful model for this type of program is the Curtin Specialist Mentoring Program (CSMP), a peer mentoring program aimed at improving well-being and academic success in universities (Siew et al. 2017, p. 1). It is a well-established program and can be used in high school and, with modification,

More information on CSMP can be found at https://students.curtin.edu.au/experience/mentoring/autism-related-conditions/

even the higher grades of elementary school. This program includes pairing an autistic student with another student who acts as a mentor. The two students meet for one hour every week to discuss issues the autistic student is having. The mentors have a weekly group meeting where they can get help if they need it. There is also an optional social group that meets every week for both mentors and mentees, in which social skills are learned as a group.

One of the main advantages of this type of program is that it can be individually tailored by the mentor for the autistic student so that they are getting help with their own specific issues. Hucklebridge hosts a similar meeting at her house on Friday nights when autistic adolescents and neurotypical young adults come to play board games. She comments that in the group, everyone—autistic and neurotypical—is able to get along, where they may not be able to get along so well in other situations.

Obviously, running a peer group is a time commitment not to be taken lightly. But the benefits far outweigh the costs and, if you are enthusiastic (or desperate), this might be the way to go. A peer group for autistic students and mentors starts with the mentor students. I suggest inviting students you know would be well-suited to mentoring another student. The meetings for the mentors start a few weeks before the peer meetings, in order to train the mentors to work with autistic students. Once you know how many mentors you have, you can invite autistic students to join the program. Each mentor works with one autistic student. Of course, you will need parental consent for the students to be involved in the program. You might need to help students set up a time for their weekly meeting and, of course, it helps to let the parents know when this meeting is so that they can remind their child about it. The meeting between you and the mentors once a week does not need to be long—30 minutes to an hour is enough time. If you have a strong team of mentors, they might also be able to plan the social hour each week. The advantages of this program include constant support, the comfort of peer-to-peer mentoring, and individualized support. The benefits for the autistic student can include increased ability in problem-solving, planning, and organizing time and academic work, and an increased knowledge about support and resources (Siew et al. 2017, p. 8). The benefits for the mentor are gaining leadership skills and learning more about autism. The benefit to the teacher is the fact that they are not doing all the work themself and sometimes—okay, many times—students come up with better solutions to problems than they would!

In younger elementary grades, you might want to run a less-formal peer mentoring program in your classroom, in which certain students are paired with autistic students for the purpose of helping them with day-to-day events. One of the common traits of autistic students is that they mimic their classmates. They are not always sure what is expected or appropriate in class, so they copy what other students are doing in order to fit in. You want to prevent them mimicking students making rude gestures—and a longer conversation with their parents later. When you pair a mentor student with an autistic student in your elementary class, you are letting your autistic student know that this is a good student to imitate. For example, when coming back from the music class, students might need to put their music folder back into their desks; the mentor student can show the autistic student what to do. You will need to let the mentor student know that they should expect to have to help the autistic student put their music folder back into their desk every time they come back from music class, and not just the first time. And it might take a while for the autistic student to remember, as difficulties with short-term memory is a common characteristic of autistic students.

Coombs relates how her son's desk was so messy at school that he missed going to a birthday party because the invitation in his desk and never made it home. Other times, an autistic student might be on the way to put the invitation in their backpack when they see Lego, play with the Lego, and leave the invitation in the Lego bin. Coombs suggests having a peer mentor help students with organization. There can be a lot of paper at school, and having someone sit beside an autistic student and help them put each piece of paper away or in their backpack, every time, can help them stay organized and make it to birthday parties! Then the autistic child feels good because a friend helped them, and the friend feels good for helping them, and the teacher feels good because she didn't have to help them! The peer mentor can also help the autistic student use their visual aids. If you have a picture on their desk of how the inside of the desk should look—say, duotangs on one side, textbooks on the other side, and the pencil case in the middle—the peer mentor can help the autistic child keep their desk looking like the visual aid. Lea uses peer mentors to help autistic students know where to go when they are on the way to music or physical education class. Further, Lea allows the autistic student some say in who they would like as a peer mentor. Giving them a choice among a few students allows them to have some control over the situation.

Lovering Spencer suggests using Tribes at the beginning of the year with the whole class. Tribes is a social-emotional learning program, with lesson plans and step-by-step processes. According to the website, Tribes aims to create a positive classroom environment where students "feel included and appreciated by peers and teachers, are respected for their different abilities, cultures, gender, interests and dreams, are actively involved in their own learning and have positive expectations from others that they will succeed." The Tribes program helps students work together and appreciate each other. As his students go through the Tribes program and discuss the issues, Lovering Spencer is able to pick who would be a good peer mentor for the autistic student.

You can find more information on Tribes at https://tribes.com/about/

What About Eye Contact?

I used to teach in a classroom right beside the Developmentally Delayed class that included autistic students. Their teacher taught the students how to greet other students and teachers in the hallway by saying hello and looking them in the eye. At the beginning of the year, very few of the students would say hello back to me when I greeted them as they passed by my classroom in the morning. By the end of the year, they would all say hello and look at me—however briefly for some, as though they were getting it out of the way so they could get back to what they wanted to do. Some would greet me in the hallways even if I didn't see them at first. By the end of the year, some were swinging by my class to say hi no matter when they walked by my room. They had mastered greetings, if not how not to interrupt.

Whether to teach eye contact or not is a controversial issue in the autistic community. Some feel that insisting on eye contact is only a way to make life more comfortable for neurotypical people while others feel that problems with eye contact cause autistic students social and professional difficulties, and so find ways to offset those dilemmas (Trevisan et al., 2017). Grandin (2013, p. 35) reports an MRI study found that the tendency to avoid eye contact might be a physical difference in the brain of autistic people. The question for teachers then becomes, *Do I teach my autistic students to make eye contact or not?* The answer is going to be found in each individual autistic student and their specific experience of eye contact.

It is easier to decide the best way to help students with more information. The more we know about eye contact and the more we know about our students, the easier it will be to help them decide on their strategy for eye contact, whether it is avoiding it altogether or finding strategies to help them with it. It could be that we give them a few strategies and they will not use them until much later in life, if at all. Some autistic people recount stories of caregivers pressuring them to maintain eye contact and how traumatic it was for them. Obviously we want to help our students, not traumatize them.

Trevisan et al. (2017) did an excellent study of first-hand accounts of how autistic people experience eye contact. The following information comes from this easy-to-read, informative article. One autistic person sums up their trouble with eye contact quintessentially by stating,

> The internal monologue starts up about whether or not I should keep looking into someone's eyes, or if I should look away [be]cause I'm creeping them out, or whether I need to look at them because they now think I'm not paying attention… (which I'm not, because I'm too busy thinking about eye contact)." (Trevisan et al., 2017, p. 10)

The first thing to understand is that there are many different reasons why autistic students avoid eye contact. Once you know the reason why your students avoid eye contact, you can either help them overcome it or help your other students understand why the autistic students do not look them in the eye. In fact, you will probably do a bit of both in most situations.

Some autistic students experience adverse reactions to eye contact, including fear, anxiety, pain, and threat responses. Many autistic people report that it is like looking directly into the sun, while others felt nausea or dizziness, or had an increased heart rate. Some students have a feeling of violation when looking others in the eyes, as though it is something only to be done with very close family or friends. They may feel exposed and might be worried about private information being unintentionally conveyed. It could be that our autistic student has sensory overload when looking in people's eyes, which takes up quite a lot of their energy and makes them tired. Some autistic students are unable to look people in the eye and focus on what they are saying at the same time, and must make a choice about which is more important. Still others feel unnatural, embarrassed, or self-conscious when looking someone in the eyes. This can be heightened by confusion about what is appropriate eye contact. Finally, autistic students might not want to maintain eye contact because they have difficulty reading information coming from our eyes and might not want to unintentionally send the wrong nonverbal information with their eyes. These are just some of the reasons autistic students might not want to look someone in the eye—there are many more. I guess if it felt like someone was sticking pins into my eyes every time I looked at someone, I wouldn't want to maintain eye contact either!

It might not always be possible to help students figure out why they do not want to look someone in the eye. They may not be that self-aware yet. One autistic person described it like this:

Making eye contact feels sort of like the first breath one takes under water using scuba gear, where there's this moment of panic as your body says, "No, no, you'll drown!" (Trevisan et al., 2017, p. 6)

Even so, if autistic students would like to be able to look people in the eye in order to overcome social and potential professional difficulties, there are many strategies suggested by other autistic people that we can teach them to help them feel more comfortable. Practicing on stuffed animals and then real animals can be an easier way to introduce eye contact, especially if there is a class pet. Some students might find it easier to look someone in the eyes if they are wearing sunglasses. Students can count to 3 or 5 in their heads when looking someone in the eyes to know how long to look before looking away, and also to distract themself from the discomfort. This strategy prevents autistic students from unintentionally staring or glaring at people, sometimes keeping them from signalling they want to fight or that they are flirting. Some autistic people suggest looking in between the eyes or just below the eye at the cheek of the other person, so that it looks like they are looking them in the eyes. Others suggest blurring your focus so that you can't really see the other person's eyes. Still others say that they look people in the eye only at the beginning of a conversation, because that is the most important time.

When autistic students are having trouble looking someone in the eyes, even though they would like to, teach them to say things to indicate they are following the conversation; e.g. "Hmmmmm," or "Oh, is that so?" or repeating what has just been said. Students can also nod their heads and smile to show they are paying attention. Some autistic people suggest positioning yourself to the side of the person who is talking instead of directly across from them so that eye contact is not as expected. And finally, others on the autism spectrum simply disclose that they are having a hard time maintaining eye contact and reassure the person that they are paying attention and they are interested in what is being said. As one autistic person said about learning to maintain eye contact, "It's useful to have people think that I'm honest and interested in what they're saying. It makes life run more smoothly" (Trevisan et al., 2017, p. 12). This is our goal for our students, that they have a good life. We want to help them to find the best way to have a successful life that is comfortable and a good fit for them.

Field Trips to the Grocery Store

One weekday I did my grocery shopping in the middle of the day (I cannot remember why I was not at work that day, but I'm sure I had a good reason!) At the checkout, I met the Developmentally Delayed class who had the classroom beside me a couple of years before. They were in the grocery store learning living skills. We were all excited to see each other and one autistic student told me they had been to the aquarium at the back of the store in the fish department to look at the fish. Another student told me in a very matter-of-fact tone that those fish were going to be eaten and they weren't really for looking at. This generated quite a bit of discussion about how sad it was and how one day they hoped to help them escape. All in all, a very exciting trip to the grocery store for both the students and me!

Many teachers and parents of autistic children talk about the importance of socializing children by teaching them living skills. In fact, it is good for all our students to learn living skills, and they can benefit from the perhaps more-detailed and repeated instruction we give autistic students. Things that other students figure out on their own, we may have to specifically teach to autistic students, or we may have to go over them more times due to short-term memory issues. It could be that autistic students remember everything we tell them (sneeze into your elbow); however, connecting it to their everyday life can be an issue (they sneeze all over us). For this reason, it is good to include living skills in as many units as possible.

Ngui tells of retraining her children hundreds of times not to run out into the street—a very important skill for our younger students! One day, their brain would just click and they would understand. Sometimes we just have to keep repeating it until they get it. It is easy to include life skills in our physical education units, as they lend themselves to safety, not to mention the health units on dental health, personal hygiene, etc.

Coombs tells of how her son's teacher had the class bake a variety of cookies. They also made a price list and signs for the cookies. Then, parents were invited to come after school to the class. They were given a bag and a price list. The parents walked around and picked out a cookie they wanted. The students tallied up the price and sold the cookies to the parents, taking the cash and making change. Math lends itself to lessons in life skills: measurement can be used in baking, addition and subtraction in making change, and fractions in dividing up pie, cake, and candies.

Hornsby describes an elementary school where students learn outside of the class as much as possible. They start every day with a 30-minute walk on a trail; they have gardens and learn how to grow food and raise chickens (just to be clear, I'm not suggesting you raise chickens at your school). The school focuses on volunteering around the community and building character. Certainly, many teachers have students grow beans in the spring, and this could be expanded to growing other vegetables. I remember doing a graph with my students of the growth of their beans. Nobody's bean did anything the first week and then, over the weekend, they shot up 10 centimetres—and then died the next day. Great graph (read in sarcastic voice). Many science units can include life-skills lessons, including lessons on plants, simple machines, and animal life.

Grandin, in a webinar for Leading Edge Seminars (2020), recommends teaching high-school students about paying bills. She suggests familiarizing students with the idea of having a budget and having to pay bills out of that budget. She proposes helping students use the adaptive technology they need in order to be able to make a budget and pay bills. In the same webinar, Grandin advocates teaching students to use YouTube to find out how to fix things when they break. I recently learned how to stop my toilet from running from YouTube and consider this an excellent life skill! The goal for teaching life skills, Ronca reminds us, is to help autistic students live independently, or as independently as possible.

I Want to Be an Astronaut

I asked Tom what advice he would give to other autistic young adults around getting a job. Tom said to tell them to research the things they are interested in outside of school and not just inside of school. Tom was interested in programming, but the courses at his high school were out of date, so he learned online. He ended up hosting a server for Minecraft. Tom learned the programming language and the server operating system himself. The job he now has is based on what he learned hosting the Minecraft server. Note for students: I did not say he played Minecraft all day for his job, but that his job was based on what he learned hosting a Minecraft server—big difference!

How can we prepare autistic students for life after school? At age 21, students have to leave school and so, as students approach this age, or sooner if possible, families start to change focus. It can be a real challenge for students and their family. Will they get a job? Will they be able to go on to college or university? As teachers, we are able to help guide and support our students as they consider all the options. Although it is not specifically our job as teachers to help prepare students for a job or for university (unless we are the guidance counsellor), it is our job to help prepare them for life. In my experience, many teachers look for opportunities to help students apply what we teach them in school to real-life situations—getting your first job at McDonalds, for example. You deserve a break today… Yes, we do!

Although there has been an increase in the number of autistic students entering university in the past few years, very few graduate (Siew, 2017, p. 2). As many jobs require a college diploma or a university degree, some autistic high-school students may want to look into various schools and we want to give them the best chance at success that we can. Often, high schools help students find a pathway and apply to colleges and universities; however, once the student graduates high school, they are on their own. It is a good idea for autistic students and families to speak with someone at colleges and universities before applying. Some post-secondary schools have excellent supports for students needing extra help, while others do not. Some schools have a week in the summer when students can come and live on campus to try it out—roommates, shared showers, cafeteria food, scary laundry rooms. Universities with peer mentoring programs, such as CSMP, might be a better choice than those that offer less support. The more support our students have when the go to college or university, the better their chances of graduating with their diploma or degree.

Working with students as young as Grade 7, start helping your students think about the kind of job they would like to have when they are older. Often, students know about only a handful of jobs, including doctor, teacher, firefighter etc., and have no idea what an actuary or a taxidermist does. Help expand their knowledge of the variety of jobs that available, especially ones that coincide with their interests. For example, a young boy who likes cars and writing might want to look into becoming an auto journalist. A young girl who likes airplanes and building with Lego might want to look into becoming an airplane mechanic. In Grandin's book *The Autistic Brain*, she lists a number of jobs students might want to look into based on the way they think (2013, p. 204–205):

- Jobs for picture thinkers: architectural and engineering drafter, photographer, animal trainer, graphic artist, jewelry designer, web designer, vet technician, auto mechanic, machine maintenance technician, theatre lighting director, landscape designer, biology teacher, plumber, welder, radiological technician, computer animator
- Jobs for word-fact thinkers: journalist, translator, librarian, copy editor, accountant, budget analyst, bookkeeper, special education teacher, speech therapist, legal researcher, historian, bank teller, tour guide

- Jobs for pattern thinkers: computer programmer, engineer, physicist, statistician, chemist, music teacher, scientific researcher, financial investing analyst, actuary, electrician

Lothian suggests that autistic high-school students try co-op programs, in which students go to a job for one semester try it out. They are volunteers at the job (sorry, no pay) and they occasionally meet with their teacher. It is common for students to work in stores, in offices, as a custodian, or with children. Sometimes the place where a student has their co-op placement will hire them when they are finished high school.

During high school, it is also possible for autistic students to get a student job, depending on their level of ability. Some common jobs done by high-school students include shovelling snow, walking dogs, mowing lawns, working in fast-food restaurants, and working in retail stores. Ahhh, this brings back memories of stocking shelves with aromatic (read smelly) candles in preparation for the Christmas rush—good times. In fact, autistic students might be better at some of these jobs than their neurotypical peers because of their attention to detail and love for routine. They will always fill the salt and pepper shakers at the restaurant and they won't forget. If students are not able to have a job, another option is to volunteer at a food bank or with a local charity; e.g., The Red Cross. This may be a good option because family members can volunteer with them. As a teacher, you can help students be aware of these possibilities and even speak with their parents about it.

In preparing students for a job, we can teach them some of the social skills they will need in the work environment. Grandin (2013, p. 195) says she has met many autistic people who have lost their jobs because they made rude comments about the appearance of their co-workers or customers. It is okay for employees to be eccentric, but not to be rude or a slob, and our students need to know that difference. At jobs, as at school, we need to be responsible for work that others want us to do and we need to work on someone else's schedule. In school, talk about this as you teach the social skills and emotional regulation that are needed in the workforce. Simply put, they can practice doing things they don't like in school in preparation for having a job, teaching them that delayed gratification pays off—usually.

Another social skill we can teach our students is how to "get in the back door." Because some autistic students can come off as eccentric in interviews, it is good to teach them how to persevere in their job search when going to interviews does not seem to work. Going to an interview might not get them a job, but solving a problem the company has could get them in the door. When talking about jobs, share stories of people we know who got jobs without going through an interview. As a teenager, I started babysitting for families who lived on my street because they knew me and then they recommended me to other families. Nowadays, people looking for an educational conference speaker find me on the Internet, through my website. A lot of jobs start this way, even for adults. Why else do we have LinkedIn accounts? Certainly not only to congratulate people on their job anniversary.

Part of our job as educators is to encourage our students to take risks—not bungee-jumping-off-the-school-roof type risks, but measured risks. Many autistic students never consider driving and, in truth, some are not able to manage such a complex skill. However, the ability to drive greatly increases the number of jobs available to them. Sometimes your job might simply be to mention opportunities that other adults in your students' lives might have never even considered. Yes, it might take longer for our autistic students to learn how to drive, but as long as the person teaching them is ready for that, it might be okay. Or it might not. Part of your job is helping your students see failure as an opportunity to learn and not as an end in itself. But how do you know you can't drive if you've never given it a good go? Not just one or two lessons, but a month of lessons. We might be surprised.

One autistic student I know would like to be a veterinarian when he grows up, and he is already an animal whisperer. His mother is helping him work toward his goal, while wondering if his sensory issues will prevent it. Already they are ahead of the game, working together to see where he could use his strengths. I am not an animal whisperer, and could use help convincing my dog not to steal my garden gloves …

Lesson Plan: Friends

How to Be a Friend

The purpose of this lesson plan is to have students explore how to make friends and how to keep friends.

"Unbelievable Unlikely Animal Friendships Compilation" on YouTube at https://youtu.be/mrudR-kIB1k is recommended.

1. Watch a video or read a book about animal friendships.
2. Hand out Friendship worksheet on page 95. Ask students to fill it out by themselves or in partners. Younger students can draw pictures instead of writing.
3. As a class, discuss the answers students wrote on the Friendship sheet. Discuss how to be a good friend. Discuss how to make a friend if you do not have any friends.

Helping Autistic Students Socialize: Checklist

Transitioning to a Mainstream Class

- ☐ Invite the autistic student to visit your classroom before they move to your class permanently.
- ☐ Invite the autistic student to come to lessons once a week or once a day before they move to your class.
- ☐ Send a couple of your students to the autistic class once or twice a week so the autistic student has friends when they come to your class.
- ☐ Take pictures of your classroom and yourself, and give them to the autistic student to look over before coming to your class permanently.
- ☐ Have the new student sit with kind, reliable students who will help them learn the schedule and know where to go and what to bring.
- ☐ Foster a sense of community in which differences are celebrated.
- ☐ Don't point out the autistic student or make them the centre of attention.
- ☐ Give them time to adjust; give yourself time to adjust.
- ☐ Have an EA or SERT come to help out one or two periods a day at the beginning.
- ☐ Include the student's interests in lessons.
- ☐ Talk with parents/previous teachers of the student to get good ideas.

Using Social Stories

- ☐ Find social stories at carolgraysocialstories.com, on Pinterest, or on YouTube, or make your own.
- ☐ Read the same social story repeatedly for the best result.
- ☐ Read Curious George and Amelia Bedelia books alongside social stories as examples of people who need extra instruction in order to understand and do things correctly.

Making Friends

- ☐ Establish an atmosphere in your classroom in which students know everyone gets the help they need and it will look different for everyone.
- ☐ Avoid giving autistic students special privileges or other students may feel jealous and avoid being their friend.
- ☐ Talk openly about difficulties people may have in conversations and how to avoid making judgments.
- ☐ Provide opportunities for students to interact.
- ☐ Make sure students know about clubs and teams they can join and encourage them to go with someone from the class.
- ☐ Inform parents of clubs and teams in the neighborhood, especially those that centre on the student's interests.
- ☐ Use social stories to help students initiate playing with another student or conversation with another student.

- ☐ Teach students to take turns playing Connect Four and use *My turn/Your turn* cards.
- ☐ Have students play board games during indoor recess to learn to take turns.
- ☐ Teach conversation skills, including the give and take of conversation.
- ☐ Identify one or two conversation skills for a student to improve upon.
- ☐ Help autistic students understand things they are doing that others may consider rude.
- ☐ Teach other students in class what to expect when being friends with someone who is autistic.

Peer Groups

- ☐ If you offer food, students are more likely come to the peer group.
- ☐ Set ground rules.
- ☐ In younger grades, run a less-formal peer mentoring program where your autistic students are paired with a peer mentor who can help them know where to go next and what to bring.

Eye Contact

- ☐ Discuss with each student whether they will work on eye contact or not.
- ☐ Have students practice on animals, wear sunglasses, count to three then look away, look between the eyes or at the cheek, blur their eyes, and look someone in the eyes only at the beginning of the conversation.
- ☐ Teach some students to say, "Oh, is that so," nod their head, position themselves beside the person, or disclose that they are having a difficult time with eye contact and reassure the person they are listening.

Preparing for College/University/a Job

- ☐ Research career interests outside school as well as in school.
- ☐ Advise parents and students to speak with someone at the college/university before applying to see what kind of support services are offered for autistic students.
- ☐ Look for post-secondary schools with peer mentoring programs.
- ☐ Teach students about a variety of jobs, especially ones that coincide with their interests.
- ☐ Encourage autistic students to do co-op in high school.
- ☐ Inform students of jobs available to high-school students.
- ☐ Encourage students to volunteer.
- ☐ Work on social skills needed in jobs.
- ☐ Teach students how to look for a "back door" into a job.
- ☐ Suggest that autistic students who are capable learn to drive.

Pembroke Publishers ©2021 *What's the Difference?* by Amanda Yuill ISBN 978-1-55138-348-4

Friendship Sheet

Friends Do

Friends Do Not

Pembroke Publishers ©2021 *What's the Difference?* by Amanda Yuill ISBN 978-1-55138-348-4

7

Helping Autistic Students Stay Safe

Help! She's Running Away!

A teacher (who gave me permission to tell this story) was on a field trip and had taken the students to the bathroom in a shopping mall. One autistic boy left the bathroom while the teacher was looking after another student, even though he was told to stay there. He had no history of running. The teacher had security look for him. He had gone up four flights of escalators to the public transportation system and had gone two stops to the south before a lady noticed he was wearing a nametag with the school's information on it; she took him to the public transportation staff. When the teacher arrived to pick up the student, the student said, "Hey, look, I made a picture of a cow."

Sometimes children run away. Some autistic children run away often. Kyriakides reminds us that autism is an invisible condition—the behavior can look willful when it is not, and we need to remind ourselves of that. Some children have to do things in a certain way—e.g., finish one thing before starting another—and if we push them to do something else, they might run away. Ngui remarks that even minor things can cause her son to have a big emotional spill and result in him running away. She reports that you can't always tell by looking at him what will happen and you can't always predict how he will react. So what can we do, as teachers, to prevent our students from running away? What can we do once they have taken off, besides putting on our running shoes?

The first thing you can do to prevent students from running away is to pick your battles. It could be that it's the end of the day and the student is tired, and it's just better to allow the student to have a bit of a break rather than clean out their desk. This is about getting to know your students—knowing how much to push and when to back off—and this only comes with time. As you get to know when your students need a break, you can offer to let them go for a short walk and then come back to the classroom. You might need to send them for that walk with a heavy backpack because they need the exercise and the sensory input.

This strategy can really cut down on the amount of running you will do—at least during school hours.

Besides picking your battles and knowing your students, there are many physical things that can help prevent students from running away. Boff encourages teachers to put a stop sign at the door as a visual reminder to students to get permission to leave the room. Meloche suggests having an alarm on the door, which might be too expensive for a school; however, you can use the bells that stores use to let them know when someone opens the door. One of my former students used to try to run away at snack time, so I would simply stand between her desk and the door during snack.

Another student I used to teach two periods a week was rarely in the classroom, because he was often running away. I saw a big improvement in him one year when he had a new teacher who had been a special education teacher and autistic class teacher in elementary schools (the year I met her she was teaching a mainstream class.) I asked her what she was doing to prevent this student from running away. She told me that she chose a favorite incentive of his. She allowed him to have the incentive if he stayed in the classroom for a very short amount of time. Slowly—very slowly—she increased the amount of time he had to stay in the classroom in order to get the incentive. Eventually, he was staying in the classroom until morning recess and then he would get the incentive. This teacher emphasized that the steps he took in order to get the incentive at first were very, very small and that the progress was very slow. She also emphasized that the teacher must be consistent—giving the incentive only when the student completes the task and then making sure the student receives the incentive—or it would take a lot longer for this system to work. This worked really well for this student, when other teachers had tried a variety of strategies that did not work. Honestly, she looked like a miracle-worker to me!

Another autistic student also often left the classroom and often got in trouble for it. When he moved to a new school, they already had a method in place for this issue. They took pictures of the five places he often ran to when he left the classroom and put them where both he and the teacher could see them. When he needed to leave the classroom, he was to take the picture of the place he was going. That way, the teacher knew where he was by process of elimination. He would take a little break and then come back to the classroom. This really cut down on the student's stress, because he knew he could take a break when he needed it and he would not get in trouble. Best of all, he got to decide where he would go.

It is a good idea to have a plan for taking autistic students on a field trip. Many parents are happy to come on the field trips (especially to places where you get to sit down a lot) and many teachers find this a good solution for students who often run away. If they are with their parent, then the student has one-on-one supervision. At times when parents are unable to come on trips, it is a good idea to find another volunteer who will come on the trip with you. Some principals will allow an EA or another teacher to go on the trip so that the student is safe and can participate. As much as possible, we want our autistic students to be able to have the same experiences as all of our students, even when it is more difficult for us. Of course, we want our students to be safe—it is our number-one consideration. For this reason, I have excellent running shoes!

While we know about incentive systems as teachers, the key for using incentives with autistic students is moving slowly and in very small steps.

See page 110 for a checklist for Helping Autistic Students Stay Safe.

Bullying Is So Old!

Two students in Grade 7 came to me because there was a group of other students who were bullying them. The other students kept teasing these two that they were dating when, in fact, they were not. They had asked the other students to stop the teasing; the bullying did not stop, but got worse. I let the two students know that I would talk with whomever they wanted me to, and they came up with a list. One recess, I called those students on the list into my classroom and told them that people were bullying these two students by saying they were dating when they were not. I reminded the students that in each bullying situation, there are three groups of people: the bullies, the bullied, and the bystanders. I said that we all knew who was being bullied and I was asking them to be the bystanders. If they heard someone teasing these two students about dating, would they stand up for them and tell the bullies to stop? Would they help the two who were being bullied to leave the situation? I did not tell the students that I knew they were the bullies. The students all agreed to be the bystanders should they witness anyone bullying these two students. I thanked them and they left. The two students let me know that the bullying stopped. Now, this might not always work, but it's a good strategy to try if you encounter bullying in your classroom.

The Bullied

Many autistic students know they are vulnerable in terms of bullying because of their quirky habits or interests (Did you know that if a bird is caught in an airplane engine, the remains that come out the back of the engine is called "snarge"?). In fact, our autistic students not only experience more-frequent bullying, but also receive less support from peers, which would work to reduce the bullying (Krieger et al. 2018, p. 10).

One of the difficulties for autistic students is that they are sometimes unconventional and the things they do can bother their classmates; for example, saying the same thing over and over, making clicking noises, etc. Other students might be trying to work and are not able to with the autistic student making noise. This can easily end up in a situation where the student is bullied. Telling the autistic student to stop won't work, because the noises are part of their autism. One strategy to try here is to have a class meeting to work on solutions. In a class meeting, many solutions could be suggested; for example, perhaps everyone could bring their own headphones into class to use while doing seat work so that the noises won't bother them. Perhaps it is possible to play white noise while the class is doing work. It is a difficult situation, because the autistic student may not want to be singled out; but if you do not find a solution, some students might bully them. If you work with parents, other teachers, and the students, even in small groups, a solution can usually be found. For example, you could set a timer for 10 minutes during which no clicking is allowed. Then, for one minute, the student can click as much as they like and anyone is welcome to join in the clicking. Then, for the next 10 minutes, there is no clicking. In an understanding class, others might join in the clicking to normalize that behavior and help the student feel accepted. This is the sort of idea we might get when we ask students and other adults to join the conversation about bullying.

Another component of an anti-bullying strategy is to talk with the student who is being bullied and ask them how you can improve the situation. Sometimes students have very good ideas about how to fix a situation that we don't think of.

For example, when one of my students kept "losing" the classroom pencils in his desk, he allowed the other students to go to his desk to get them out when there were no classroom pencils left in the box. They would ask him if they could look in his desk and he would give them permission and they would pull out four or five pencils. Problem fixed, with no teacher intervention.

The Bully

What also needs consideration is when the autistic student seems to be bullying others. They might insist that they get to use a certain resource and, when others use it, they might take it by force. Alternatively, the autistic student might be frustrated or triggered by something that happens in class, and that might result in their using physical force against another student. Welker reminds us that behavior is communication. If we can find out why the autistic student engages in such behavior, we can help them make better choices the next time (e.g., to not dump the shavings from the pencil sharpener onto the floor). Of course, part of helping them make better choices is to enforce consistent consequences, and to make sure students know ahead of time the expectations for the classroom and the consequences for not following those expectations.

One thing to watch out for is children triggering the autistic student on purpose to see them explode or get into trouble. One teacher noticed students would go by an autistic student's desk and knock things off it. The autistic student would get very angry and use physical force, and then he would get into trouble. It looked like the autistic student was bullying these students; in actual fact, it was the opposite. Once the teacher realized what was going on, she was able to address the issue. Often, students are reticent to tell the teacher what is going on and it is important to be explicit about the difference between things it is important to tell the teacher and things you try to work out on your own. I usually tell my students that after they have tried to work it out on their own once, they should come to me the second time they encounter the same problem. It is important to encourage students to let us know if they are being bullied, including experiencing cyberbullying (online bullying), as students often keep this to themselves.

One day, I was teaching a Grade 1/2 class the first step of conflict resolution when someone is bullying you: *State the problem*. I was teaching the students to say, "Stop it! I don't like that," in a strong voice. I was having students practice using their strong voice, and one little boy was having a difficult time finding his strong voice. He whispered, "Stop it! I don't like that." So I demonstrated how to say it with a louder voice. As this was an impromptu lesson after recess, we were still in the hallway and had not yet gone into the classroom. We happened to be right outside the caretaker's office. After a couple of minutes of the lesson, the caretaker came out of his office and, in his very loud voice, demonstrated how to firmly say, "Stop it! I don't like that!" The students all laughed.

Sometimes autistic students will not know how to resolve conflict when they have it, or will try to resolve it in ways that simply lead to more bullying. Here are three easy steps you can teach students to follow when they encounter bullying:

1. First, teach students to identify and state the problem; e.g., *I don't like it when you hit me.*
2. Secondly, have students negotiate a solution. In younger grades, the solution could simply be that they will tell the teacher when it happens. As students

get older, they can try to find out from the other student why the behavior is happening. Perhaps the other student is tired of the clicking noise and so they pushed the autistic student. Students can negotiate a solution that works for both of them. They may ask the teacher to put their desks far away from each other so that the other student can't hear the clicking noise. The student who pushed the autistic student can agree to use their words to ask that the clicking noise stop.

3. The final step is to enforce the agreement. Both students can remind each other of the agreed upon solution. You might need to go over these steps, demonstrating and helping your autistic students many times, as conflict resolution is a social skill that may not come naturally to them. (To be honest, I think many Canadians need help being a bit more vigorous with our conflict resolution—it can be done well and politely! I know we are a people with a leaf on our flag and a beaver as our national animal; all the same, we can use our strong voices now and then!)

As we foster a classroom atmosphere in which everyone is accepted for who they are, with all their differences, we can give students tools they need to deal with many social issues, including bullying. This is especially important for our autistic students, as bullying is almost certainly an issue for them. We can make our anti-bullying policies clear and explain how we are going to implement them in order to contribute to a sense of security for our autistic students. We can have an online classroom where students post things and talk with both the teacher and other students. Students who email friends and who talk with friends on social media have more positive friendships (Krieger, 2018, p. 10), which can prevent bullying. We can talk about the desire to fit in and the desire to have friends. I always say that as long as each student has one friend in class, they will be okay.

Things They Don't Teach You in Teachers' College

I don't know about you, but we were definitely not told in teachers' college that students might try to harm themselves, harm others, or engage in sexual touching. We weren't taught how to deal with that. Of course, I went to teachers' college quite a while ago, so maybe things have changed. I have learned quite a few practical strategies as a teacher. I remember one staff meeting where we discussed how to keep students from kissing and heavy petting during recess. I hope you won't encounter such extreme situations; however, if you do, this section might be of some help.

Students Who Self-Harm

If, like me, you were totally unprepared for students who harm themselves, Ngui reassures us that we can't always rectify troublesome behavior immediately because, in a class of 30 students, some things take time. She encourages us not to judge a child by their behavior, but to see the behavior as the child trying to tell us something and a prompt for us to dig down to the root of the behavior. This is a theme that I have heard repeated over and over by parents, teachers, and specialists: autistic children do not behave badly because they want to, but because they are communicating something to us. Usually it is, "I don't want to do this." When harming themselves, some students hit themselves, bang their head against something, bite themselves, or, even more seriously, cut themselves with knives or stab themselves with pencils, forks, etc. Our job is to find out why and to help them find other options to deal with these problems.

Of course, of course, we are going to try to stop them from hurting themselves. We are going to try to take away the pencil, knife, fork, or whatever they are using as a weapon; we are going to put a mat between their head and the wall; we are going to distract them and use their favorite things to calm them down. If needed, we're going to call the office for help, or perhaps bring in an EA or a Special Education teacher who is listed on their safety plan. At all times, it is important to remember that we also need to stay safe. When we are helping a student who is self-harming, it is important to remember to stay safe ourselves.

Lothian tells of a student who would start to hit herself, and then would escalate to throwing things at people. Of course, one of the difficulties is that, even if the autistic student is normally very expressive, they might not be able to tell us what is wrong when they are so worked up. Some students do not even remember what they did when they were angry. As Lothian got to know this student, she could recognize the student's triggers and head off escalating behavior. If the student started to hit herself, it was a sign that things were escalating, so Lothian would remove her from the classroom and take her down the hall in order to calm down. The autism team from the school board put together a program for the student, based on her needs and diagnosis. As Lothian followed the program, which included rewards, the student improved. By the end of the semester, the student was able to stay in class the whole time, doing the same tasks as the rest of the class.

Steve Edelson, a researcher and Director of the Autism Research Institute in the United States, realized that autistic people who self-harm might be attempting to moderate the effects of overstimulation and various sensory issues (Silberman, 2015, p. 333). If this is the case, as we help our students ascertain what is causing them to be overstimulated, we can help decrease the stimulation and, as a result, the self-injurious behavior. This issue is disturbing because, as teachers, we do not want to see our students hurt and we do not want to see them hurting themselves. It is especially difficult when we are not able to convince students to stop the self-harming behavior. We might require help from the office or from another educator who has a relationship with our student. In the most difficult of cases, we could have to call the parents to come if we are not able to stop the behavior. This is not defeat. This is just how it is some days with autistic students. It's okay. Remind yourself that it's okay.

Students Who Harm Others

While some students harm themselves in order to communicate or in reaction to overwhelming stimuli, other students harm teachers or their classmates. One teacher told me he had a student who threw a chair at him a few times when she was very upset. One time, when this student tried to bite through the teacher's nipple, the EA put her arm in the way and the EA's arm was bit, saving the teacher's nipple. Many teachers have stories of students who have exhibited violent behavior in the classroom. In fact, the Elementary Teachers Federation of Ontario found that 70% of their teachers had personally experienced violence and witnessed violence against another staff person in the 2018 All-Member Workplace Survey. Therefore, it is important to be ready to handle violent situations in the classroom. Having a plan can make the difference between defusing

It's a good idea to look into the resources available from your board of education. Many boards have autism teams or special education teams that will come to help in extreme cases. If your student is self-harming, there is a good chance you can get help.

the situation and the situation getting out of control. Of course, the most important thing in these situations is keeping everyone—other students, yourself, and the student who is being violent—safe.

The Ontario College of Teachers, in their 2016 special advisory on Safety in Learning Environments, advises teachers to "make responsible decisions as would a careful or prudent parent or guardian" (p. 1). When possible, you are going to stop children from being hurt as a careful parent would. For example, one of my Kindergarten students was going to jump out a classroom window. We were not on the ground floor. Although we are warned not to touch the children, I pulled her away from the window (she was halfway out it already) and shut the window. As a loving teacher acting as a careful parent, I could not let her fall to the ground and hurt herself. On the other hand, I had two Grade 7 boys in a fist fight in my music classroom one day. I did not get in the middle of it, but used my teacher voice to tell them to stop. Luckily, they did stop. However, I would not have put myself into the middle of their fight; it would not have been safe. It is important to remember that, if we are hurt, we are not able to help others.

The first thing we can do is to prevent students from harming other people through forming a good relationship with the student. Coombs recommends embracing our students' strengths and reinforcing the behavior we prefer to see in our classrooms; e.g., "I like seeing you working so well with your protractor." We can make sure we have fun in the class, by telling funny stories, gross facts, or ghost stories (but not too-scary ghost stories, because I sometimes get nightmares, and so do some of the students). I like telling gross facts: Did you know that the greater short-horned lizard squirts blood out of its eyes as a defense mechanism? Kids love it!

Another way to prevent harmful situations is to be aware. When you start a school year, you don't know your students very well, and this can be a dangerous thing. It is important to read over students' records to see if they have a safety plan, and to update that plan with any educator who is going to work with that student in the current school year. The music and physical education teachers will thank you for it. It is also important to be aware of body language. Are your student's neck and face getting redder? Is their voice getting louder? Are they gesturing larger? Do they have clenched fists or a clenched jaw? Are they doing the rooster walk (neck out, hands on hips)? If you see these signs, start de-escalating the situation. Sometimes autistic students are not able to get off a certain behavior track once they have started on it. If they are headed toward the point where they will be unable to turn back, you want to prevent them from getting there.

When you see students getting upset, use some de-escalation strategies. First of all, remain calm. It sounds so easy, doesn't it? It is probably one of the most difficult things teachers do. When someone has just spit on you, sworn at you, or kicked you, it is very difficult to remain calm. However, if you want to de-escalate the situation, that is what you have to do. Take a breath and speak in a nonthreatening tone, using nonjudgmental words. You can ice your leg later. Also make sure to protect your own triggers. Many teachers are triggered when students swear at them, so it might help to remind yourself that it is not personal. The student is reacting not only to what has just happened, but also to other things that have accumulated over the years and have not been properly addressed. If you allow students to see that they can upset you by swearing at you, every time they want you to be upset, they will swear at you. Being calm helps them and it helps you.

Give the student space. Take a step back and make sure that other students are also giving them space. Sometimes the other students are tired of having interruptions over and over in class and, when a situation starts, they gang up on the student who is having difficulties, telling them to stop and sit down (and often calling them various, not complimentary, names). This does not help and only escalates the situation. As the teacher, make sure that everyone is giving your student space so that they can calm down.

Avoiding a power struggle is another key to de-escalating the situation. Don't argue with the student; instead, just ignore challenging questions. Use short answers and phrases. Rather than stating what you don't want them to do, simply restate what you want them to do; e.g., "Please sit down at your desk." Validating the student's feelings can also help to avoid a power struggle. Tell them that you understand that they are feeling angry, and that it is okay to feel angry. It helps to use the word "we" instead of "you" to show them you are including them in your class; e.g. "I'm sure we can work this out." It also can help if you can get them to say, "yes"; e.g. , "I think you are angry, is that right?" It is difficult to be aggressive when you are agreeing with someone. Another strategy to avoid a power struggle is to apologize. You don't have to apologize for being wrong, especially if you were not wrong. However, you can say, "I'm so sorry that there was no snack left," or "I'm sorry someone vandalized your locker." Many students tend to soften up when someone apologizes to them, especially when they know they have done something wrong, too, like try to poke you with a mathematical compass.

Distraction is another good de-escalation technique. I find this works really well with younger students. If I ask them to help me with something, they often forget that they were mad about something, and I get help folding the letters to go home that night. This is not to say that I won't address the violent or harmful behavior later; it just means that I need them to be calm before I can talk with them about it, and distraction is one way to achieve that. If you simply offer the student another activity, they might be able to do that activity calmly, and you can avoid a violent incident.

One of my favorite de-escalation strategies is giving the student choices. I often give the student a choice of going to the office to calm down or going to the bathroom, getting a drink, and coming back in 5 to 10 minutes. I find many, many students take the option to go for a little walk to calm down. I give them a note or hall pass so they won't get in trouble, and note the time they should return to the classroom.

If a student is very angry, I sometimes give them the choice of listening to music on their phone or a class computer (with headphones, of course). Usually, I don't allow phones to be used in the classroom; however, this effective way of calming students down works when many other strategies don't, especially with older students. I might offer a choice of sitting in the book corner and reading a book or sitting with a friend who can help them calm down. Some teachers protest that this is simply rewarding the student for bad behavior. Actually, this is preventing a violent situation. These are strategies to prevent violence and, as we get to know our students, we will know when these strategies are needed and when they are not.

If, despite your best efforts, the student does proceed to hurt others or become violent, the first thing to do as a teacher is to get help. Other students might be able to help, especially the friends of the student who is being violent. They might be able to convince the student to go for a walk and calm down. Other students can also go to enlist the help of a nearby teacher or a teacher who has a good relationship with the student; e.g., the special education teacher, the gym teacher, or a favorite EA. Having another teacher in the room could help. Of course, you can get help from the office, and this is often in the safety plan. If a student is throwing things, it might be necessary for you and other students to clear the classroom and wait in the hall (taking your purse and laptop with you). If you are unable to get help from anyone, it might be necessary to take the whole class to the office, where at least there will be another adult (i.e., the office administrator) observing the situation. If you do this, make sure all the students come with you.

You do not need permission from the office to call 911. If someone is in danger, you can call 911 or the police, even before calling the office. You are responsible for the safety of everyone in your classroom, including yourself. When I was presenting a workshop, one teacher told me that she was in a portable when two boys started a very serious fist fight. She called the office but nobody came to help, so she called 911. A police officer came and broke up the fight, but the two students who had been fighting started taunting the officer, so the officer called for backup. There were two police officers in the portable before anyone came from the office. Sometimes there can be two or more situations in a school and only one principal available to deal with them. It is best to have a plan and be prepared.

After a violent incident in which a student harmed themself or somebody else, be sure to write down what happened on the forms provided by your board of education: violent incident forms, workplace compensation (if you were harmed), etc. Even if the principal or other teachers tell you that this happens all the time and there's no need to fill out a form, fill it out anyway—even when it takes you an hour to find them online. The forms protect you. Take a copy of the form or a screenshot if it is online. Keep the copy of the form in your files. One time a Kindergarten student fell off the monkey bars and hurt herself. I insisted the office call home because it was a bad fall, even though the administrator did not want to. I also filled out a form. The next day it turned out that the student had broken her arm. It is always better to be safe than sorry. Fill out the forms; keep a copy.

The next thing to do after a violent incident is to talk with your union representative, health and safety representative, or whoever represents you at the school in this situation. It is good to let them know what happened so that, if a parent or principal comes to them, they will know the story. They can also provide resources that you might not know about; for example, counselling services that are covered by the school board for this type of situation. I know, I know, you are thinking this is becoming too big a deal for a small situation. Again, if someone is hurt in the situation or even threatened, it is better to be safe than sorry. There could be an investigation into the incident at a much later date. It is best to have covered all your bases at the time it happened. I assure you, your union representative or health and safety representative will not think you are overreacting; they will think you are being wise. And you *are* being wise.

Processing what happened could take some time, depending on the severity of the situation. It is okay to take the next day off in order to recover. Often the gravity of the situation doesn't hit until much later when the shock wears off. It's good to talk with friends and a counsellor. It is also important to talk with the class about what happened and allow them to process as well. Some students might feel unsafe or not want to be in the same classroom as the student who was violent. It is important to address these very real and significant issues. Of course, it is also important to talk with the student who was violent or harmful to decide together what can be done to prevent the situation from happening again.

After talking seriously with your students, it is good to end the conversation on a lighter note and joke a bit with them. Why didn't the skeleton cross the road? Because he didn't have the guts.

I highly recommend forgiving the student. Do you know any teachers who are bitter and not good teachers anymore because of their bitterness? I do, too. I don't want to become like them, so I try to forgive my students. They don't have to ask for forgiveness, I just offer it to them in my heart. Okay, okay, that might sound hokey, but if I hold onto the anger, it prevents me from having a better relationship with the student in the future. I don't mean that I give them permission to be harmful. I mean I do not hold the matter against them. I may have to forgive them over and over, every time it comes to my mind. People always tell me forgiving the student lets the student "off the hook." I have some bad news for these people. The student is already "off the hook"; they have received the consequence and they have forgotten about it and moved on. We're the ones on the hook because we are still upset. I forgive to let myself off the hook.

Obviously, we want to prevent harmful and violent situations from happening at all. One of the best ways to do this is to prevent the student from being triggered. This involves getting to know the student and observing what triggers them. For this reason, Cook recommends keeping an ABC chart when a student is habitually harmful: ABC chart stands for Antecedent, Behavior, and Consequence. When an incident happens, as soon as possible, write down what caused the incident or what happened just before the incident. Also take note of the behavior and any consequences given. Every time the same behavior happens, write it down. This way, if there is a pattern or a trigger, you might be able to find it. Also, you can see from the record which consequences worked, and what time of day or month it tends to happen. There's a reason teachers are wary of full moons… A lot of information can be gleaned from an ABC chart that can help you to help your students. The OCT's Safety in Learning Environments (2016, p. 7) states that "Safety is a precursor to learning." Our goal is that all students are safe and learning, including our autistic students, who might sometimes harm others. We do not want to be sending them home all the time; we want to find other strategies to help them to be calm in school and prevent them from being triggered.

If you try all these strategies and find that none of them works, I recommend Ross W. Greene's book, *Lost and Found: Helping Behaviorally Challenging Students (and, While You're At It, All the Others)* for a more in-depth strategy that has worked in many schools and juvenile prisons.

You Are What You Eat

I would be remiss if I did not mention one more thing that could help decrease challenging behavior in the classroom. Many educators and parents talk about large, almost miraculous, changes in their autistic child/student when their diet was changed. Some autistic children have Leaky Gut Syndrome, where partially digested food leaks from the digestive system through cracks into the tissue beneath it. One of the treatments for Leaky Gut Syndrome includes a healthy diet and avoiding processed foods (Campos, 2019). Whether the student has Leaky Gut Syndrome, has allergies, or simply would benefit from a healthy diet, it could be a good idea to mention to their parents that a healthy diet can help lead to a change in behavior (and even a change in the ability to communicate, according to some parents).

Students Who Engage in Sexual Touching

For sure, I don't remember the class in teachers' college where they taught us how to deal with students sexually touching themselves and others. I used to teach in a swim program; teachers would bring in their classes and we would teach them to swim. An autism class came once a week. Some of the boys would stand in front of the water jets in the pool until they had erections. Their teacher was always after them to move away from the jets. Then I was supposed to teach them back float? I know of one high-school boy who would always pull down his pants or walk around naked. Another autistic boy who went around grabbing the female students' breasts. Because the subject is taboo and people are embarrassed, there is very little teaching on it. So what do you do when your students are sexually touching themselves or others?

Ronca asserts that there is always a function to the behavior and, if we can find out the function, we can eliminate or reduce those behaviors. In the same way that we try to find out why students are behaving in violent ways, we can try to find out why they are using sexual touching. Some common functions are task avoidance, attention seeking, and sensory issues. One of the most effective methods of task avoidance I have seen by a student is simply starting to take off their clothes. Everyone would forget the student wasn't doing the task and would start focusing on getting the student's clothes back on. He had great fun and got lots of attention! Especially when he would run out to the front of the school, which was on a busy street. It's a miracle there weren't more accidents in front of that school! So the first thing to do is to see if you can provide positive attention to your students, and to ensure incentives for finishing tasks are repeated and enticing enough to prevent sexual touching as an attention-seeking behavior.

Of course, then we come to the obvious answer. Students touch themselves and others due to sensory-seeking behavior; in other words, because it feels good. Hucklebridge adds that it can be a matter of self-medication through stimulation for things such as depression, which can also involve a lack of impulse control. In this case, it is a matter of teaching our students what is and is not appropriate to do in public. Talking with parents before having a talk with the student about this issue might help you know if you are introducing a completely new idea or if the student is already aware of acceptable behavior. It is advisable to have a teacher of the same gender as the student have a talk with them, and to have more than one teacher in the room during the talk. It is best to use a matter-of-fact tone of voice and the proper vocabulary for body parts; e.g. breasts, not boobs. Let the students know that touching their penis, vagina, or breasts is not something we do in public, nor at school. You might have to tell them quite a few times. Hucklebridge also recommends teaching students that it is not okay to touch anybody else's penis, vagina, or breasts without their permission, and then it should also be in private. You might have to use incentives and consequences to ensure their behavior, much as you would if you want them to walk in the hall instead of run. Most of your autistic students will not think that this subject is taboo, nor will they be embarrassed about it, because that is a social construct and, by definition, many autistic people have trouble understanding social norms.

If you are having difficulty, involving other teachers and the parents in these conversations can help. Usually, health is taught by the physical education teacher, and they can be more used to talking with students about sexual issues. They may be able to help, especially if they already teach the student P.E. The parents are most likely dealing with the same issues when they go out in public as

It might seem unlikely, but the issue of stopping sexual touching at school will eventually become like all the other regular parts of the day. It is simply one more thing you work on with your student in order to help them have the best life they can have.

a family. It is good to join forces with the parents so that the student is receiving the same message at home and at school.

Autistic Burnout Is a Thing

There was an autistic student who came into high school and made new friends, wanting a fresh start. The problem was that he felt like they weren't real friends because he wasn't really being himself—he was trying to be "normal." Trying to be something he wasn't exhausted him to the point that at the end of the day he was not able to do his homework. Part of the trouble for this boy was that he was worried he would not have friends if he was himself. Similarly, Lea taught a student with Asperger's who was able to keep up with his classmates academically but who was an outsider socially. She comments that, interestingly, the other students in the class would not allow him to be himself. Many autistic people know the pain of rejection for being who they are. This can lead to masking, also called masquerading or camouflaging. These are strategies used by autistic students to compensate for their differences in order to fit in or conform to expectations. For example, autistic students might try to stop or control their repeated language or rocking; they might try to imitate other students' speech and behavior; etc. This, in turn, can lead to Autistic Burnout, sometimes also called Autistic Regression. According to the well-titled article, "Having All of Your Internal Resources Exhausted Beyond Measure and Being Left with No Clean-Up Crew: Defining Autistic Burnout":

> [Autistic Burnout] is a syndrome conceptualized as resulting from chronic life stress and a mismatch of expectations and abilities without adequate supports. It is characterized by pervasive, long-term (typically 3+ months) exhaustion, loss of function, and reduced tolerance to stimulus. (Raymaker et al., 2020, p. 2)

Much of the information on Autistic Burnout comes from the article by Raymaker et al.

What this means is that students who are masking their autistic characteristics will eventually be exhausted, unable to do work or even care for themselves, and will not be able to protect themselves from sensory overload at all; e.g., they will have to wear dark sunglasses all the time to stop the light from hurting their eyes. You might notice that a student who had formerly been accused of "copying" other students, even buying the same Star Wars T-shirt and hanging around them, now no longer cares and sits by themself all the time. Obviously, this is something we want to help our students avoid.

The desire to remake oneself is common problem among young adults as they transition from high school to college/university or a job. Therefore, students in their last year of high school are especially vulnerable to Autistic Burnout. Further complicating the syndrome is the fact that, when autistic people report what they are experiencing, they are often told that their problems are their own fault or they are dismissed. This can lead to students questioning their own sense of reality, an eroded self-esteem, an increase in anxiety, and an increase in suicidal thoughts, making the issue even worse.

One of the best things you can do to prevent your students from experiencing Autistic Burnout is to cultivate an accepting class atmosphere. As you encourage students to recognize that everyone is unique, you can foster an attitude of acceptance, empathy, and support, while addressing issues of discrimination and stigma. When autistic students feel accepted for who they are, it goes a long way toward preventing future difficulties. Fostering an accepting atmosphere can include helping students recognize why some people might need more time alone than others. I remember living in Japan and working very hard all day to fit in with the culture; I would come home at night and just watch funny, old movies in English online in order to recuperate. Thank you, Tom Hanks.

More than simply accepting our autistic students, we can teach them healthy boundaries and how to negotiate and maintain those boundaries. The ability to say no, to self-advocate, and to negotiate their own limits with external demands are skills that all your students need and ones that can be taught to everyone in your class; e.g., "No, I'm not going to clean up the class hamster's cage for you." It can be helpful to allow autistic students to go to the reading corner more often than others in order to be in a quiet place by themselves. It is good to help your students recognize their limits and then to understand what will replenish them when they are nearing those limits; e.g., time alone, exercise, decreasing or increasing sensory input, etc. They might need a couple of days and not a couple of hours alone in the reading corner in order to recover from an extended period of masking.

There are many peer support groups online if there are none in your area. The online resource wrongplanet.net has forums on general autism, school and college, and love and dating.

Part of preventing Autistic Burnout and then treating it is making sure autistic students have adequate support. There tends to be more support for elementary students than for high-school students, and it is important to consult with parents, special education teachers, and community organizations in order to offer autistic students an option for support that suits them, and their specific needs and personality. Especially important is making sure they are part of a peer support group for autistic students, because validation of feelings and experience from other autistic students can be very healing and encouraging. Your goal is to help every student be themselves and find friends in class who allow them to be themselves. If you can help prevent masking by your autistic students, you can help prevent Autistic Burnout.

Lesson Plan: Calming Challenging Behaviors

Learn to Defuse

The purpose of this lesson plan is to help students acquire a variety of strategies to help themselves and others calm down when their behavior is challenging.

1. Read *The Most Magnificent Thing* by Ashley Spires. If you do not have this book in your library, readings of it are available on YouTube.
2. Discuss what it looks like when people explode.
3. Discuss how we can calm down when we explode.
4. Discuss how we can help someone calm down when they explode.

Make Tableaux

1. Explain that a tableau is like a picture of a scene. Instead of people acting out the scene, they remain still.
2. With the whole class, make a tableau of the scene from *The Most Magnificent Thing* in which Ashley explodes.
3. Divide students into groups and ask them to make their own tableaux of someone exploding.
4. Ask the groups to make a tableau of helping the person who is exploding to calm down.
5. Ask each group to share their tableau with the class.

Helping Autistic Students Stay Safe: Checklist

Running Away
- ☐ Pick your battles; sometimes it is okay to let the student do what they want/need to do instead of doing what we would prefer.
- ☐ Get to know students and their triggers.
- ☐ Make sure students get enough exercise.
- ☐ Put a stop sign on the door.
- ☐ Put a bell or alarm on the door that sounds when it is opened.
- ☐ Use incentive programs with very small, incremental steps.
- ☐ Allow students to leave the room when they need a break, as long as you know where they are going.
- ☐ Set a time limit for their being out of the room.
- ☐ Have parents or another staff member accompany the child on a field trip.

Bullying
- ☐ Ask the bullies to become the bystanders who help those being bullied.
- ☐ Foster an accepting atmosphere in your class in which people can forge friendships that can help protect them from bullying.
- ☐ Have a class meeting to address bullying issues.
- ☐ Work with parents, other teachers, and students to find a way to address the bullying.
- ☐ When the autistic student is bullying others, remember that behavior is communication and look for the source or reason for the behavior.
- ☐ Learn the autistic student's triggers and help them calm down before they reach their breaking point.
- ☐ Teach students to try to work out issues between themselves before coming to you for help.
- ☐ Have online class discussion rooms where positive connections are encouraged.

Students Who Self-Harm
- ☐ Try to figure out what the student is trying to communicate through self-harm.
- ☐ Confiscate any weapons and call for help from an EA or the office.
- ☐ Be sure to stay safe and keep students safe.
- ☐ Recognize triggers to prevent self-harm.
- ☐ Get help from the autism or special education team of your board of education.
- ☐ Decrease sensory stimulation.

Students Who Harm Others
- ☐ Have a plan to keep everyone safe in dangerous situations.
- ☐ Form a good relationship with the student to prevent harmful behavior.
- ☐ Use positive reinforcement and encouragement.
- ☐ Be aware of safety plans and discuss them with other teachers.

- ☐ Be aware of escalating body language.
- ☐ Use de-escalation strategies, including remaining calm.
- ☐ Protect your own triggers.
- ☐ Give the student space.
- ☐ Avoid a power struggle.
- ☐ Don't argue or engage.
- ☐ Use the word "we" instead of "you."
- ☐ Get the student to agree with you.
- ☐ Apologize to the student.
- ☐ Distract the student.
- ☐ Give the student a choice.
- ☐ In a violent situation, get help from other students, other teachers, or the office.
- ☐ Clear the room if the student is throwing objects.
- ☐ Call 911 if you think you or the students are in danger; you do not need permission from the office to do this.
- ☐ Write down what happened on the school forms and keep a copy for yourself.
- ☐ Talk with your union representative or your health and safety representative.
- ☐ Take time to process what happened; take time off if you need it.
- ☐ Allow students to talk about the incident and reassure them.
- ☐ Forgive the student.
- ☐ If violent incidents happen often, make an ABC (Antecedent/Behavior/Consequence) chart to find out what is instigating them and what consequences are working.

Students Who Engage in Sexual Touching
- ☐ Look for the function of the sexual touching in order to help reduce/eliminate it.
- ☐ Give students a lot of positive attention to avoid attention seeking.
- ☐ Ensure incentives for finishing tasks are enticing.
- ☐ Teach students sexual touching is inappropriate in public.
- ☐ Teach students they need permission to touch someone else's penis, vagina, or breasts, and then it needs to be done in private.
- ☐ Offer incentives and consequences to help students learn the preferred behavior.

Autistic Burnout
- ☐ Cultivate an inclusive class atmosphere.
- ☐ Teach students healthy boundaries and how to enforce them.
- ☐ Allow autistic students time to re-energize.
- ☐ Make sure autistic students have adequate support.
- ☐ Encourage autistic students to join a peer mentoring program.

Pembroke Publishers ©2021 *What's the Difference?* by Amanda Yuill ISBN 978-1-55138-348-4

Last Words: Worth it All

As I interviewed people while preparing to write this book, I heard over and over how many educators really love working with autistic students. Here are just a few quotes from them:

> I really love the kids with autism. I have a place in my heart for them. They are special because they have so much to offer—it's just a matter of bringing them out of themselves. It's all about having a relationship with them. — Nancy Lothian

> I've always had a heart for these kids and they make a beeline for me. Many times, students were assigned to different EAs but they ended up with me. It is God's gift he gave me but also I find the most incredible passion and interest working with them. — Barbie Schiller

> I love kids with autism. I love them. They are creative usually. They see the world in different ways. I still run into kids I taught. I still get an Easter Bundt [cake] from the parents of a student I taught more than 10 years ago. When you do a good job, treat the kids with love and respect, they will come back. It really makes a huge difference in their lives. — Rob Lovering Spencer

As we work with autistic students integrated into our classes, we, like these educators, will come to love these students as we love all our students. They do offer us many challenges and opportunities to grow. They make us better educators. As we teach autistic students, we learn more about them, about ourselves, about the kind of teachers we want to be, about the kind of people we want to be, and about the kind of society we want to be.

When we see our autistic students, and all our students, as unique and not disabled, we can see that, "individuals with ASD are not disabled by their impairments, but more by the dominant societal attitudes of what is considered 'normal'" (Siew et al., 2017, p. 14). And we can help change these attitudes by increasing what is included in the definition of normal in our classrooms and, over time, in society. The goal is not to teach a disabled student, but to teach a student.

I wrote this book to help teachers with their autistic students. I interviewed 24 people and read dozens of books and scholarly articles, went to workshops and conferences, and used my experience of teaching many autistic students integrated into my classes. When I finished writing the book, I realized that it's not a book about teaching autistic kids; it's just a book about teaching kids.

As we learn how to teach our autistic students, we learn how to be better teachers for all of our students. Yes, it is more work. Anything worthwhile takes effort and time. On the difficult days, it is okay to just make it through the day. As we look back at our week or month or years with our autistic students and we see how much they improved, how much our other students learned, and how much we have learned ourselves, we will see that it is worth it. It really is worth it.

Acknowledgments

List of Interviewees

To prepare for writing this book, I interviewed 24 people about their involvement with autism and autistic people. Throughout the book, I refer to them and their experiences.

Mary Boff: Special education teacher, former educational assistant in elementary school

Janice Cook: Child and youth worker, employment coach, Instructor Therapist, mother of an autistic child

April Coombs: Mother of an autistic child

Sarah Cronin: Special Education Program Lead in a high school, special education teacher

Beth Cubitt: Mother of two autistic children

Joseph Hancock: Young adult with Asperger Syndrome

Katy Hornsby: Mother of two autistic children

Sue Hucklebridge: Durham College ASD Specialist, Royal Conservatory ASD Specialist, mother of two autistic children

Kathy Kohlemeier: Mother of an autistic child

Eva Kyriakides: Special Education Advisory Committee Chair for a board of education

Sari Lansimaki: Former educator in elementary school

Gillian Lea: Vice-principal, special education teacher in elementary school

Nancy Lothian: Educational Assistant in elementary and high schools

Rob Lovering Spencer: Special education teacher in an elementary school

Bailey Mandic: Autistic young adult, son of Trina Meloche

Tharsiga Manikandan: Special needs assistant in elementary and high schools

Trina Meloche: Mother of two autistic children, including Bailey Mandic

Emily Ngui: Mother of two autistic children

Sunita Rathee: Educational assistant in an elementary school

Joseph Ronca: Autism class teacher, special education teacher in an elementary school

Barbie Schiller: Educational assistant in a high school

Danielle Soo Lum: Autism class teacher, special education teacher in an elementary school
Tom: Young adult with Asperger Syndrome
Lori Ann Welker: Mother of an autistic child

I really like this tradition of thanking people who have helped you with the book in the book itself! What a great idea! I have many people to thank.

First and foremost, I would like to thank God for answering my many, many prayers about this book.

A thank-you to Mary Macchiusi and everyone at Pembroke Publishers for your continued support and encouragement, and for answering my many questions when I call and email. I also so enjoy being able to drop by for a chat every now and then! Thank you, Kat Mototsune, for editing the book and for knowing which stories I have used in which books and not allowing me to repeat myself. Thank you for making sure I am writing what I mean to say!

Many people gave me their time so I could interview them in preparation for writing this book. Thank you for answering my questions—and even emailing me later with more tidbits! Thank you to Mary Boff, Janice Cook, Jennifer Cook, April Coombs, Wilma Craik, Sarah Cronin, Beth Cubitt, Joseph Hancock, Katy Hornsby, Sue Hucklebridge, Kathy Kohlemeier, Eva Kyriakides, Sari Lansimaki, Gillian Lea, Nancy Lothian, Emily Ngui, Rob Lovering Spencer, Bailey Mandic, Tharsiga Manikandan, Trina Meloche, Sunita Rathee, Joseph Ronca, Barbie Schiller, Danielle Soo Lum, Lori Ann Welker, and Tom. I hope I have been able to capture the passion with which you related your stories to me. Thank you, Cathy Cocker, for putting me in touch with so many of these experts!

To the many school communities where I have worked, thank you for accepting me as part of your community and teaching me so much during my time with you. Thank you to the students, parents, staff, and administrators, many of whom I count as friends, at Birch Cliff Heights, Brimwood Public School, Clairlea Public School, Don Mills Middle School, Ionview Public School, Kahoku Junior High School, Maryvale Public School, Tredway-Woodsworth Public School, Wexford Public School, and many more.

Thank you, Nicki Diak, Lindsay Dwarka, and Alicia DesMarteau for offering your expertise to help make this book better. Your ideas, tips, and suggestions for changes truly are appreciated. Thank you, too, to the many friends who were always interested in how the book was coming along, for listening and offering encouragement, prayers, and suggestions!

My family are my greatest supporters and encourage me more than they know. Thank you to my brother Mathieu and his wife Alison, and their boys Connor, Isaac and Emmett; to my sister Cindy and her husband Scott, and their girls Ainsley and Morgan; and to my mom Pat. Thank you for listening when I read out sections of the book and for giving suggestions, ideas, opinions, and love.

Professional Resources

References

Asperger, H. (1991). "'Autistic psychopathy' in childhood" (U. Frith, Trans.). In U. Frith (Ed.), *Autism and Asperger Syndrome*. Cambridge, UK: Cambridge University Press.

Autism Speaks Canada. *PDD-NOS*. https://www.autismspeaks.ca/about-autism/ what-is-autism/pdd-nos/

Autism Speaks, *What Is Autism?* https://www.autismspeaks.org/what-autism

Blume, H. (1997, June 30). "Autistics are communicating in cyberspace" *New York Times*. https://archive.nytimes.com/www.nytimes.com/library/cyber/ techcol/063097techcol.html

Brown, I. & Radford, J. P. (2015). "The growth and decline of institutions for people with developmental disabilities in Ontario: 1876–2009" *Journal on Developmental Disabilities, 21*(2), 7-27. http://oadd.org/wp-content/ uploads/2015/01/41021_JoDD_21-2_v23f_7-27_Brown_and_Radford.pdf

Campos, M. (2019, October 22). *Leaky gut: What is it, and what does it mean for you?* Harvard Health Publishing: Harvard Medical School. https://www.health.harvard.edu/blog/ leaky-gut-what-is-it-and-what-does-it-mean-for-you-2017092212451

Cantiani, C., Choudhury, N. A., Yu, Y. H., Shafer, V. L., Schwartz, R. G. & Benasich, A. A. (2016). "From sensory perception to lexical-semantic processing: An ERP study in non-verbal children with autism" *PLoS One, 11* (8), 1-31. doi:10.1371/journal.pone.0161637 https://journals.plos.org/ plosone/article/file?id=10.1371/journal.pone.0161637&type=printable

The Council of the Ontario College of Teachers. (2016, March 3). *Safety in learning environments: A shared responsibility: Professional advisory.* Retrieved 2020, September 14. https://www.oct.ca/-/media/PDF/ Advisory%20Safety%202013/2013_professional_adv_en_web2.pdf

Cullen, T & Ricker, C. (2016). *Josiah's fire: Autism stole his words, God gave him a voice*. Savage, MN: Broadstreet Publishing Group.

Curtin University. (n.d). *Autism and related conditions mentoring.* Retrieved 2020, September 18, from https://students.curtin.edu.au/experience/mentoring/autism-related-conditions/

Dawson, M. (2004, January 18). *The misbehaviour of behaviourists: Ethical challenges to the autism-ABA industry.* Sentex. https://www.sentex.ca/~nexus23/naa_aba.html

ETFO All-Member Workplace Survey Results. (2018) Elementary Teachers' Federation of Ontario. Retrieved 2020, September 18, from https://www.etfo.ca/AboutETFO/MediaRoom/MediaReleases/Shared%20Documents/ViolenceSurvey.pdf

Goodall, C. (2020, January 21). *How to teach autistic pupils… by autistic pupils.* Tes. https://www.tes.com/news/how-teach-autistic-pupilsby-autistic-pupils?fbclid=IwAR1901Wh2819Ijh1h74IRWHkIRE9EDdzSohEisEmFNY8fWs7PaYjQfQeZp8

Goodall, C. (2018). "Inclusion is a feeling, not a place: a qualitative study exploring autistic young people's conceptualisations of inclusion" *International Journal of Inclusive education. 24*(12), 1285–1310.

Grandin, T. (2020, May 26). *Practical tips for helping children and young people on the spectrum during the pandemic* (Online Webinar). Toronto, ON: Leading Edge Seminars.

Grandin, T. (2013). *The autistic brain: Helping different kinds of minds succeed.* Boston, MA: Houghton Mifflin Harcourt.

Gray, C. (2020). Social story sampler. *Carol Gray Social Stories.* Retrieved 2020, September 18, from https://carolgraysocialstories.com/social-stories/social-story-sampler/

Greene, R.W. (2016). *Lost & found: Helping behaviorally challenging students (and, while you're at it, all the others).* San Francisco. CA: Jossey-Bass.

Habib, A., Harris L., Pollick F. & Melville C. (2019). "A meta-analysis of working memory in individuals with autism spectrum disorders" *PLoS ONE, 14*(4), 1-25. https://doi.org/10.1371/journal.pone.0216198

Hoopmann, K. (2006). *All Cats Are on the Autism Spectrum.* London, UK: Jessica Kingsley Publishers.

Kluth, P. & Schwarz, P. (2008). *Just give him the whale: 20 ways to use fascinations, areas of expertise, and strengths to support students with autism.* Baltimore, MD: Paul Brookes Publishing.

Kohn, A. (2020, January 21). *New research adds to an already compelling case against ABA.* https://www.alfiekohn.org/blogs/autism/

Krieger, B., Piškur, B., Schulze, C., Jakobs, U., Beurskens, A. & Moser, A. (2018). *Supporting and hindering environments for participation of adolescents diagnosed with autism spectrum disorder: A scoping review.* PLoS ONE, 13(8), 1–30. https://doi.org/10.1371/journal.pone.0202071

Mastrangelo, S. (2009). "Harnessing the power of play: Opportunities for children with autism spectrum disorders" *Teaching Exceptional Children, 42* (1), 34–44. https://doi.org/10.1177/004005990904200104

Mastrangelo, S. (2019, October 23). *Reframing autism spectrum disorder: Possibilities for educator practice* [Conference session], Special Education Information Sharing Forum/Chiefs of Ontario, Thunder Bay, ON.

Morneau Shepell Children's Support Solutions. *ABA vs IBI: What is the difference?* https://childrensupportsolutions.com/aba-vs-ibi-what-is-the-difference/

Murphy, S. (2019). *Fostering mindfulness: Building skills that students need to manage their attention, emotions, and behavior in classrooms and beyond.* Markham, ON: Pembroke.

National Autistic Society. (2020, August 21). *Social stories and comic strip conversations.* Retrieved 2020, September 18, from https://www.autism.org.uk/about/strategies/social-stories-comic-strips.aspx

Plank, A. & Grover, D. (2004, July 1). *Autistic teens create website for people with Asperger's Syndrome.* PRWeb. https://www.prweb.com/releases/2004/07/prweb137362.htm

PricewaterhouseCoopers (2006). *Market for disabled children' services: A review.* PwC.

Psychology Today. *Asperger's Syndrome.* https://www.psychologytoday.com/ca/conditions/aspergers

Raymaker, D. M., Teo, A. R., Steckler, N.A., Lentz, B., Scharer, M. Santos, A. D., Kapp, S. K., Hunter, M, Joyce, A. & Nicolaidis, C. (2020). "Having all of your internal resources exhausted beyond measure and being left with no clean-up crew: Defining autistic burnout" *Autism in Adulthood, 2*(2), 132–143. http://doi.org/10.1089/aut.2019.0079

Robison, J. E. (2007). *Look Me in the Eye: My Life with Asperger's.* New York, NY: Three Rivers Press.

Sacks, O. (1993, December 27). "An Anthropologist on Mars" *The New Yorker.* https://www.newyorker.com/magazine/1993/12/27/anthropologist-mars

Shanker, S. (2012). *Calm, Alert and Learning: Classroom strategies for self-regulation.* North York, ON: Pearson Education Canada.

Siew, C. T., Mazzucchelli, T. G., Rooney, R. & Girdler, S. (2017). "A specialist peer mentoring program for university students on the autism spectrum: A pilot study" *PLoS ONE 12*(7), 1–18. https://doi.org/10.1371/journal.pone.0180854

Silberman, S. (2015). *NeuroTribes: The Legacy of Autism and Future of Neurodiversity.* New York, NY: Avery Publishing.

Surrey Place.(n.d.) *Intensive Behavioural Intervention.* Retrieved September 14, 2020, from https://www.surreyplace.ca/services-provided/intensive-behavioural-intervention/

Tammet, D. (2006). *Born on a blue day: A memoir of Asperger's and an extraordinary mind.* New York, NY: Free Press.

Tanaka, H., Negoro, H., Iwasaka, H., Nakamura, S. (2017) "Embodied conversational agents for multimodal automated social skills training in people with autism spectrum disorders" *PLoS ONE 12*(8), 1-15. https://doi.org/10.1371/journal.pone.0182151

Tobik, A. K. D. (2020, January 15)."Social stories for kids with autism – The ultimate guide" *Autism Parenting Magazine.* https://www.autismparentingmagazine.com/social-stories-for-autistic-children/

Trevisan, D. A., Roberts, N., Lin, C. & Birmingham, E. (2017) "How do adults and teens with self-declared Autism Spectrum Disorder experience eye contact? A qualitative analysis of first-hand accounts" *PLoS ONE 12*(11), 1–22. https://doi.org/10.1371/journal.pone.0188446

Williams, D. (1996). *Autism: An inside-out approach.* London, UK: Jessica Kingsley Publishers.

Winter-Messiers, M.A. (2007). "From Tarantulas to toilet brushes: Understanding to special interest areas of children and youth with

Asperger syndrome" *Remedial and Special Education, 28*(3), 140–152. https://journals.sagepub.com/doi/10.1177/07419325070280030301

The Zones of Regulation. *The Original Framework Designed to Foster Self-Regulation and Emotional Control.* https://www.zonesofregulation.com/index.html

Recommended Resources

Children's Books

Hoopmann, K. (2006). *All Cats Have Asperger Syndrome.* London, UK: Jessica Kingsley Publishers.

Land, C. (2017). *The Superhero Brain: Explaining autism to empower kids.* Self-published.

Lears, L. (1998). *Ian's Walk: A story about autism.* Park Ridge, IL: Albert Whitman & Company.

Mosca, J. F. & Rieley, D. (2019). *The Girl Who Thought in Pictures: The story of Dr. Temple Grandin.* Seattle, WA: The Innovation Press.

Newson, K. & Hindley, K. (2019). *The same but different too.* London, UK: Nosy Crow Ltd.

Novels

Arnold, E. (2017). *A Boy Called Bat.* New York, NY: HarperCollins.

Arnold, E. (2018). *Bat and the Waiting Game.* New York, NY: HarperCollins.

Benjamin, A. (2015) *The Thing about Jellyfish.* New York, NY: Little, Brown and Company.

Burley, R. F. (2017). *Mouse.* Winston-Salem, NC: Prospective Pres.

Haddon, M. (2003). *The Curious Incident of the Dog in the Night-time.* Toronto, ON: Random House Canada.

Lord, C. (2006). *Rules.* New York, NY: Scholastic.

Martin, A. M. (2014). *Rain Reign.* New York, NY: Feiwel and Friends.

Biographies/Autogiographies

Barron, J. & Barron, S. (1992). *There's a Boy in Here: Emerging from the bonds of autism.* Arlington, TX: Future Horizons.

Fling, E. R. (2000). *Eating an Artichoke: A mother's perspective on Asperger Syndrome.* London, UK: Jessica Kingsley Publishers.

Grandin, T. (2006). *Thinking in Pictures, expanded edition: My life with autism.* New York, NY: Vintage Books.

Isaacson, R. (2009). *The Horse Boy.* New York, NY: Little, Brown and Company.

Maurice, C. (1993). *Let Me Hear Your Voice: A family's triumph over autism.* New York, NY: Ballantine Books.

Mont, D. (2001). *A Different Kind of Boy.* London, UK: Jessica Kingsley Publishers.

Park, C. C. (1982). *The Siege: The first eight years of an autistic child.* Gerards Cross: UK: Colin Smythe.

Park, C. C. (1982). *The Siege: A family's journey into the world of an autistic child.* New York, NY: Back Bay Books.

Park, C. C. (2001). *Exiting Nirvana: A daughter's life with autism.* New York, NY: Back Bay Books.

Perry, S. P. (2015). *Sand in my Sandwich: And other motherhood messes I'm learning to love.* Ada, MI: Revell.

Prince-Hughes, D. (2004). *Songs of the Gorilla Nation: My journey through autism.* New York, NY: Three Rivers Press.

Robison, J. E. (2011). *Be Different: adventures of a free-range Aspergian.* Toronto, ON: Doubleday Canada.

Robison, J. E. (2016). *Switched On: A Memoir of brain change and emotional awakening.* New York, NY: Spiegel & Grau.

Senator, S. (2005). *Making Peace with Autism: One family's story of struggle, discovery, and unexpected gifts.* Durban, SA: Trumpeter.

Seroussi, K. (2002). *Unraveling the Mystery of Autism and Pervasive Developmental Disorder: A mother's story of research and recovery.* New York, NY: Harmony Books.

Williams, D. (1992). *Nobody Nowhere: The remarkable autobiography of an autistic girl.* New York, NY: Doubleday.

Nonfiction

Armstrong, T. (2002). *You're Smarter Than You Think: a kid's guide to multiple intelligences.* Minneapolis, MN: Free Spirit Publishing.

Attwood, T. (2006). *The Complete Guide to Asperger's Syndrome.* London, UK: Jessica Kingsley Publishers.

Bailey, B. A. (2011). *Managing Emotional Mayhem.* Oviedo, FL: Conscious Discipline.

Bascom, J. (Ed.). (2012). *Loud Hands: Autistic people, speaking.* Washington, DC: Autistic Self Advocacy Network.

Bashe, P. R. & Kirby, B. L. (2005). *The Oasis Guide to Asperger Syndrome: Advice, support, insight and inspiration.* New York, NY: Crown Publishers.

Eberly, S. (2001). *365 Manners Kids Should Know: Games, activities, and other fun ways to help children learn etiquette.* New York, NY: Harmony Books.

Gray, C. (2010). *The New Social Story Book: Over 150 social stories that teach everyday social skills to children with autism or Asperger's Syndrome, and their peers.* Arlington, TX: Future Horizons.

Dymond, K. (2020). *The Autism Lens: Everything teachers need to connect with students, build confidence, and promote classroom learning.* Markham, ON: Pembroke.

MacDonald, F. & Sawler, S. (2018). *Be Prepared!: The Frankie MacDonald guide to life, the weather, and everything.* Halifax, NS: Nimbus Publishing.

Sacks, O. (1998) *The Man Who Mistook His Wife for a Hat and other clinical tales.* New York, NY: Touchstone.

Sacks, O. (1995). *An Anthropologist on Mars: Seven paradoxical tales.* New York, NY: Alfred A. Knopf.

Shearer, A. (1981). *Disability: Whose Handicap?* Hoboken, NJ: Blackwell Publishers.

Siegel, D. J. & Bryson, T. P. (2011). *The Whole-brain Child: 12 revolutionary strategies to nurture your child's developing mind.* New York, NY: Delacorte Press.

Tashie, C., Shapiro-Barnard, S. & Rossetti, Z. (2006). *Seeing the Charade: What we need to do and undo to make friendships happen.* Nottingham, UK: Inclusive Solutions.

Yuill, A. (2018) *Reaching and Teaching Them All: Making quick and lasting connections with every student in your classroom.* Markham, ON: Pembroke.

Online Resources

The Forgotten History of Autism https://youtu.be/_MBiP3G2Pzc
Nipissing District Developmental Screen https://www.uottawa.ca/health/sites/www.uottawa.ca.health/files/g_18m_eng_cdn_sample.pdf
Temple Grandin, Ph.D. templegrandin.com
The Autism Community in Action https://tacanow.org
Thinking Person's Guide to Autism http://www.thinkingautismguide.com
The UDL Guidelines http://udlguidelines.cast.org
Wrong Planet wrongplanet.net

Organizations

Academic Autistic Spectrum Partnership in Research and Education (AASPIRE) https://aaspire.org
Autism Society of America www.autism-society.org
Autism Speaks www.autismspeaks.org
Autistic Self Advocacy Network https://autisticadvocacy.org
Geneva Centre for Autism www.autism.net
Global and Regional Asperger Syndrome Partnership www.grasp.org

Index